Paige Muller | Andrea Seiger

22 Walks in Washington, DC That You Must Not Miss

Photographs by Shedrick Pelt

emons:

To my friends and family, for feeding my curiosity. PM
To all the storytellers I know, have met, and have yet to meet. AS

© Emons Verlag GmbH
Cäcilienstraße 48, 50667 Köln
info@emons-verlag.de
All rights reserved
© Photographs by Shedrick Pelt, except:
p. 52: Andrea Seiger (Neon House);
p. 76: Andrea Seiger (Ching Ching Cha Tea House)
© Cover icons: shutterstock/olegtoka, shutterstock/bigkai,
shutterstock/OlgaChernyak, adobestock/Tekin,
adobestock/Mine Eyes Design, adobestock/Budi
Cover layout: Karolin Meinert
Layout: Editorial Design & Art Direction, Conny Laue,
based on a design by Lübbeke | Naumann | Thoben and Nina Schäfer
Maps: altancicek.design, www.altancicek.de
Basic cartographical information from Openstreetmap,
© OpenStreetMap-Mitwirkende, OdbL
Edited by: Karen E. Seiger
Printing and binding: Grafisches Centrum Cuno, Calbe
Printed in Germany 2025
ISBN 978-3-7408-1987-3
First edition

Guidebooks for Locals & Experienced Travelers
Join us in uncovering new places around the world at
www.111places.com

Foreword

Have you ever walked out your door and turned in an unplanned direction? Any time is a wonderful time to do just that, and where better than in your own city?

The two of us, along with any friends who come along, have been known to trip over one another when we see something that sparks our curiosity, like a historic sign, a mural, or an architectural flourish. We speculate, we exchange what we know, we look up details we want to know, and then we venture on to the next wonder. It is with this boundless curiosity and interest in the uncommon that we explore together and on our own, and it is in this vein that we have created these walks through DC's well-known and lesser-known neighborhoods.

Talking to strangers is one of the joys of exploring. Through them, we have discovered stories that are surprising or new to us, even in the neighborhoods we thought we knew so well. Perfect strangers have told us of ancestors, neighbors, shops, buildings, scandals, and favorite places. The long conversations and shared laughter always propel us further into our endless urban odyssey.

We find joy in attending performances and supporting our favorite small businesses. We notice the scents and colors of gardens and parks, and we are reminded that our rivers really do flow with history. And we have found kinship with people we have only encountered at their own gravesites. Through the lens of a keen-eyed photographer, we often see a new dimension of the places we have included.

With this book as your guide, step through a door that is ajar or an open gate, or head down an enticing alley. Look for things you have never noticed close to home, or visit a neighborhood you've never seen. Fear nothing. Enjoy everything.

We fully intend to keep walking, and we invite you to join us as we continue to seek out new stories and new adventures in this extraordinary place we call home.

22 Walks

1. Alexander Hamilton Walk
   Musical inspiration from stage to sidewalk | 6

2. All That Jazz Walk
   Explore Duke Ellington's life in DC | 14

3. Art Deco Walk
   Stories of beautiful buildings and their residents | 26

4. Avenue of the Presidents Walk
   Diplomatic & cultural spots with a bit of scandal | 36

5. City Summit Walk
   Ingenuity in the highest neighborhood in DC | 48

6. Creatives at Work Walk
   Art, shops, and neighborhood vibes | 58

7. Flags of Embassies Walk
   International stories through the history of flags | 66

8. Food Lovers Walk
   Tantalizing tour of culinary diversity | 80

9. Frederick Douglass Walk
   Trace his impact and legacy through his footsteps | 90

10. Forgotten Georgetown Walk
    Hidden history of a lost Black community | 100

11. Grand Hotels Walk
    History, ghosts, and radiant decor | 110

12. Hidden Alley Houses Walk
    Secrets of these backstreet spaces revealed | 120

13   Latino at Heart Walk
Latin American culture thriving since the 1950s | 134

14   Lincoln's Ghost Walk
Imagine the president enjoying his old 'hood today | 146

15   Locomotion History Walk
We sure have gotten around | 156

16   Native Americans Walk
Leaders came to DC on business; some never left | 166

17   Nouveau Riche & Strivers Walk
Gilded Age excess coexisting with Black excellence | 176

18   Riverfront Walk
Lore of the Nation's River | 186

19   Secret Gardens Walk
Charming outdoor spaces and quiet oases | 200

20   Soul of the City Walk
Proud entrepreneurs and grand restorations prevail | 208

21   Urban Renewal Design Walk
A neighborhood's roots before the bulldozers | 218

22   Wardman Architecture Walk
History behind the designs of famed DC architect | 228

DOWNTOWN DC NW

1 Alexander Hamilton Walk
Musical inspiration from stage to sidewalk

> BEST TIME: Any season or time of day
> DISTANCE: Approximately 2 miles
> ROUTE DESCRIPTION: Easy walk through busy downtown streets – mind the traffic lights.
> START: Metro at Archives-Navy Memorial-Penn Quarter (Green, Yellow Lines)
> END: Metro at Metro Center (Blue, Orange, Red, Silver Lines)

Thanks to Lin-Manuel Miranda's Broadway musical smash hit *Hamilton*, former Treasury Secretary Alexander Hamilton (1757–1804) has never been more famous. Much of *Hamilton* takes place in New York City, but there is a great deal of his history in the District. Even though he never lived here, his legacy and ambition can be traced from the page to the stage to the streets where "History Has Its Eyes on You."

There's no better place to start a walk centered on one of the Founding Fathers than at the ❶ NATIONAL ARCHIVES, the nation's record keeper. Among the founding documents here is the U.S. Constitution. Hamilton served as one of New York's delegates to the Constitutional Convention at Philadelphia in 1787. Head toward 7th Street NW and turn left. After a short walk, turn left onto F Street NW. The ❷ SMITHSONIAN NATIONAL PORTRAIT GALLERY has a portrait of Hamilton (1806) by John Trumbull that has been on permanent display since 1979. You may have a copy of this image in your possession right now; its likeness is printed on the US 10-dollar bill.

Next, continue on F Street NW and turn right on 9th Street NW to the next corner to the ❸ MARTIN LUTHER KING JR. MEMORIAL LIBRARY is on the corner. You can check out a copy of Pulitzer Prize-winning author Ron Chernow's landmark biography

Opposite: General Marquis de Lafayette Statue

Above: Martin Luther King Jr. Library rooftop
Below: Dolley Madison House on Lafayette Square

Alexander Hamilton here. It was Chernow's work that fueled and inspired the hip-hop musical.

Turn left on G Street NW, then right on 12th Street NW. At New York Avenue NW turn left to the ❹ NATIONAL MUSEUM OF WOMEN IN THE ARTS (NMWA) on the next corner. When it opened in 1981, NMWA became the world's first major museum to focus strictly on championing the work of women artists. The museum's collection features 5,000 works from the 16th century to the present created by more than 1,000 artists, including Mary Cassatt, Frida Kahlo, Alma Thomas, Lee Krasner, Judy Chicago, Amy Sherald, and many others. Take a moment to reflect on Hamilton's wife Elizabeth Schuyler Hamilton, who is credited with preserving the legacy of her husband. In the musical's finale, her character sings the song, "Who Lives, Who Dies, Who Tells Your Story," in which she reveals all the efforts she made to tell her husband's story. Without Eliza's efforts, Hamilton's biography, and by extension the musical, might not have been realized.

Fork right on H Street NW. Eliza Hamilton frequented the "President's Neighborhood" and was a friend of her neighbor Dolley Madison. The former First Lady and wife of James Madison lived in the yellow ❺ DOLLEY MADISON HOUSE on the corner of H Street and Madison Place. Dolley joined Eliza in advocating and raising money for a monument to Hamilton's mentor and friend George Washington. Since the mid-19th century, witnesses have claimed to have seen Dolley's ghost rocking in a chair where the porch used to be and smiling at passersby.

To the left is Lafayette Square where you'll find statues of Master General Marquis de Lafayette (1757–1834) and other military comrades Hamilton knew during the Revolutionary War. Head toward the intersection of Jackson Place and H Street NW. ❻ DECATUR HOUSE, on the corner, has been a fixture since 1818, making it one of the oldest surviving homes in the city. It's also one of the few remaining examples of slave quarters in the District and of Black people who were held "in bondage in sight of the White House," according to the White House Historical Association. Growing up on an island near a Caribbean waterfront frequented by ships transporting enslaved people from Africa, Hamilton was no stranger to the realities of slavery.

Turn left and toward the corner of Pennsylvania Avenue and Jackson Place NW near the White House. On the left is a statue of ❽ **GENERAL JEAN-BAPTISTE DONATIEN DE VIMEUR,** Comte De Rochambeau (1725–1807), who gets a shoutout in the *Hamilton* musical. An ally of the American cause, his name served as a codeword at the battle of Yorktown, where he commanded the French troops.

Hamilton as we know it may not have been created if it wasn't for the 2009 Poetry Jam at ❾ **THE WHITE HOUSE.** Lin-Manuel Miranda debuted an early version of *Alexander Hamilton* before it was even intended to be a musical. Then President Barack Obama and First Lady Michelle Obama were literally in the "Room Where It Happens."

Cross the park to the left to the statue of ❾ **GENERAL MARQUIS DE LAFAYETTE** (1757–1834). In the musical, Lafayette is first seen at the beginning of Act One, where he is introduced to a 19-year-old Alexander Hamilton, a new immigrant from the Caribbean. He and Hamilton become close friends and Revolutionary allies. Next door to the White House is the ❿ **US TREASURY DEPARTMENT BUILDING,** which has occupied the same site since 1800. Hamilton was the first secretary of the Treasury, serving under President George Washington (1732–1799) and helped lay the foundation for the country's financial system.

Walk to 15th Street NW, turn right, and go to Alexander Hamilton Place NW, a short distance away. A ⓫ **STATUE OF ALEXANDER HAMILTON** stands in front of the south wing of the Treasury Building. Access to the statue is restricted by a fence, but you can see it clearly from the sidewalk. Charles Atlas, an Italian-born American who was the most popular bodybuilder of his day in the 1920s, was the model for the statue.

Cross 15th Street NW, turn left to F Street NW, and turn right at the corner. ⓬ **THE HAMILTON,** an eclectic, late-night eatery

Clockwise from top left: White House; US National Archives; Alexander Hamilton statue; window; The Hamilton restaurant; National Museum of Women in the Arts

and music venue, pays homage to its namesake with a cheeky image of Alexander Hamilton in shades. If you're feeling "young, scrappy, and hungry," order the Hamilton burger and a mule for a tasty way to unwind after this historic journey.

❶ NATIONAL ARCHIVES
700 Pennsylvania Avenue NW
Washington, DC 20408
www.archives.gov

❷ SMITHSONIAN NATIONAL PORTRAIT GALLERY
8th & F Streets NW
Washington, DC 20001
npg.si.edu

❸ MARTIN LUTHER KING JR. MEMORIAL LIBRARY
901 G Street NW
Washington, DC 20001
www.dclibrary.org/mlk

❹ NATIONAL MUSEUM OF WOMEN IN THE ARTS (NMWA)
1250 New York Avenue NW
Washington, DC 20005
www.nmwa.org

❺ DOLLEY MADISON HOUSE
1520 H Street NW
Washington, DC 20005
www.whitehousehistory.org/dolley-madison-house-on-lafayette-square

❻ DECATUR HOUSE
748 Jackson Place NW
Washington, DC 20006
www.whitehousehistory.org/decatur-house

❼ GENERAL JEAN-BAPTISTE DONATIEN DE VIMEUR
Southwest corner of Lafayette Square
Pennsylvania Avenue &
Jackson Place NW
Washington, DC 20001
www.nps.gov/whho/learn/historyculture/rochambeau.htm

❽ THE WHITE HOUSE
1600 Pennsylvania Avenue NW
Washington, DC 20500
www.whitehouse.gov

❾ GENERAL MARQUIS DE LAFAYETTE STATUE
Southeast Corner of Lafayette Square
Pennsylvania Avenue &
Madison Place NW
Washington, DC 20001
www.nps.gov/places/000/general-lafayette-statue.htm

❿ US TREASURY DEPARTMENT BUILDING
1500 Pennsylvania Avenue NW
Washington, DC 20220
home.treasury.gov

⓫ STATUE OF ALEXANDER HAMILTON
Alexander Hamilton Place NW
Washington, DC 20005
home.treasury.gov/south-plaza-hamilton-statue

⓬ THE HAMILTON
600 14th Street NW
Washington, DC 20005
www.thehamiltondc.com

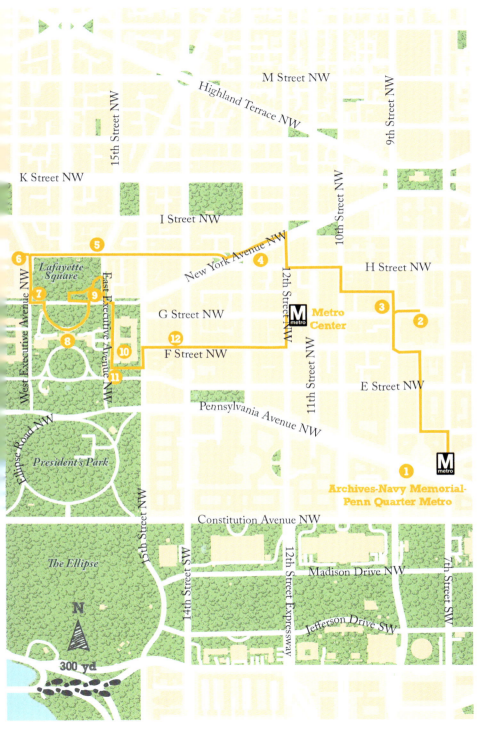

2 — All That Jazz Walk
Explore Duke Ellington's life in DC

> **BEST TIME:** Any season or time of day
> **DISTANCE:** 1 mile
> **ROUTE DESCRIPTION:** Easy walk with historic stops
> **START:** Metro at U Street/African-American Civil War/Cardozo (Green Line)
> **END:** Metro at Shaw-Howard University (Green Line)

The name Duke Ellington (1899–1974) is practically synonymous with DC. While the jazz legend gained fame at Harlem's Cotton Club in New York City, his legend began here in his hometown. On some of his first recordings, Duke Ellington's band is called the Washingtonians. You can't "Take the A Train" in DC, but there is a bridge and high school named for him.

Before he moved to Harlem in 1923, Ellington's life and early career were centered in the Shaw neighborhood where he grew up. As racial segregation increased, Shaw became a "city within a city" and the heart of Black Washington. It is often called "Black Broadway" because of the number of jazz and night clubs that were clustered along U Street. It was also the center of Black culture in the United States before the Harlem Renaissance began, attracting some of the leading Black intellectuals of the day.

The ❶ **THURGOOD MARSHALL CENTER FOR SERVICE AND HERITAGE** was the nation's first YMCA for African-Americans and was a vital neighborhood hub. Ellington was affiliated with it, as was poet Langston Hughes (1901–1967), who lived here in the early 1920s. Today, the building is named in honor of Thurgood Marshall (1908–1993), the first Black Supreme Court Justice, who strategized here with other lawyers on the landmark 1954 school desegregation case.

Opposite: Duke Ellington *Encore* statue

Clockwise from top left: Duke Ellington's childhood home; the original Ben's Chilli Bowl; neighborhood street; Lincoln Theatre; Industrial Bank of Washington

Make your way to S Street NW, turn right, then turn right on 13th Street NW. Ellington lived on this street from age 11 to 18 at ❷ 1805 13TH STREET NW (1910–1914) and across the street at ❷ 1816 13TH STREET NW (1915–1917). While living here, he soaked up the rich musical traditions of the neighborhood. Continue walking to the Whitelaw Apartments.

Opened in 1919, the ❸ WHITELAW HOTEL was the first luxury apartment hotel created for a Black clientele in DC – look up to see the name still engraved above the entrance. Known as the "Embassy," it was financed by Black investors, built entirely by Black Americans and designed by Isaiah T. Hatton (1883–1921), one of the nation's first Black architects. Ellington and other musicians who played on U Street were frequent guests. Continue on to U Street NW and turn right.

"Black Broadway" was the heartbeat of Shaw. By 1920, more than 300 Black-owned businesses operated in the area. Old-timers said U Street was so grand that you had to wear a tie if you were going to come here. In the 1930s and 1940s, the likes of Cab Calloway, Pearl Bailey, Sarah Vaughan, and the Duke played on U Street and hung out at after-hours clubs.

Next, you'll cross U Street NW and turn right at the corner. ❹ THE LINCOLN THEATRE was a cultural center of DC that predated and influenced the Harlem Renaissance. From the day it opened in 1922, the theatre was important to the Black community because it was managed by Black people. Behind it was the Lincoln Colonnade, a dance hall that hosted all the big bands of the day. President Franklin D. Roosevelt held his birthday parties there, and Ellington and Pearl Bailey were joined by nationally acclaimed artists like Billie Holiday, Nat King Cole, Cab Calloway, and Louis Armstrong.

There is a mural on the wall of the Lincoln Theatre honoring ❺ NEGRO LEAGUE BASEBALL and trailblazing players Mamie "Peanut" Johnson (1935–2017) and Josh Gibson (1911–2047). In 1953, Johnson became the first female player to pitch in the Negro leagues, and was one of only three women ever to play for the league. Gibson, a 12-time Negro Leagues All-Star, became the second

Negro League player to be inducted into the National Baseball Hall of Fame, in 1972. Ellington played baseball in his youth and recounted in his memoir how President Teddy Roosevelt used to watch him and the neighborhood kids play ball. Ellington was such a baseball fan that he might not have discovered his talent for the piano if it wasn't for a fluke accident that ended his baseball dreams.

Next door is the famous ❸ **BEN'S CHILI BOWL.** Among many other Black performers, Ellington dropped by when his concert tours brought him back to DC. It was opened in 1958 by Ben and Virginia Ali. During the 1968 riots after the assassination of Martin Luther King, Jr., Ben's was the only business on U Street that was able to stay open after curfew, feeding protesters and police alike, who found common ground in mouth-watering bowls of chili. Today, the restaurant is a must-visit spot. The walls are covered in photographs of its famous visitors, including George Clinton, Mary J. Blige, Chris Rock, and Anthony Bourdain. It was even Barack Obama's restaurant of choice during the days before his 2009 inauguration.

Head to U and 12th Streets NW. The building across the Street to your right is the ❹ **TRUE REFORMERS BUILDING.** Completed in 1903, it was among the grandest structures in the US to have been designed, built, and financed by Black Americans. It was designed by John A. Lankford (1874–1946), DC's first registered Black architect. The building was the setting for many community social and civic organizations for Shaw residents. Ellington played one of his first paid performances with his band Duke's Serenaders in one of the ballrooms.

❺ **INDUSTRIAL BANK OF WASHINGTON,** at 11th Street to your left, was founded in 1913 by entrepreneur John Whitelaw Lewis. Like the Whitelaw Hotel, it was built by Isaiah T. Hatton (1883–1921). When it opened, Industrial was the only Black-owned bank in the District. A majority of the Black-owned businesses on U Street were established with loans from this bank. Customers included Ellington, heavyweight champion Joe Louis, and singers Sarah Vaughan and Nat King Cole.

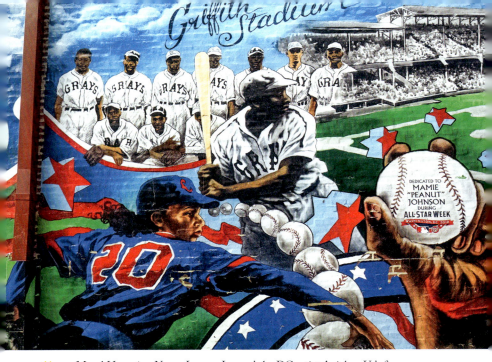

Above: Mural Honoring Negro League Legends by DC artist Aniekan Udofia
Below: Duke Ellington mural on the True Reformer Building

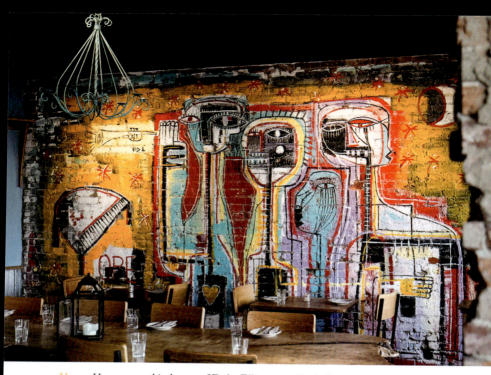

Above: *Homage* mural in honor of Duke Ellington at Right Proper Brewing Company
Below: Washington Conservatory of Music and School of Expression

You can't miss the building with the decorative piano keys across the street. ❾ BOHEMIAN CAVERNS was originally a Prohibition-era speakeasy that was remodeled to look like a cave, complete with plaster stalactites. It was a major site in the development of the jazz tradition that started in the 1920s. Over the years, it showcased performers including Ellington, Louis Armstrong, Miles Davis, and Thelonious Monk. The club was also known to jazz aficionados as the spot where pianist Ramsey Lewis (1935–2022) recorded his Grammy-winning single "The In Crowd" in 1965. A new business now occupies the space, with only the decorative exterior hinting at its musical past.

From here, stroll to the U Street Metro station. On the corner is the ❿ PRINCE HALL MASONIC TEMPLE. Founded in 1825 by enslaved and free Black people, it was headquarters for the nation's earliest and largest Black fraternity. Named in honor of Prince Hall, a Revolutionary War veteran known as the first African American Mason, the building was an important social and cultural center and also boasted a bowling alley, a ballroom, and a restaurant. Some of the musicians who played here were Masons themselves, including Ellington, Nat King Cole (1919–1965) and Count Basie (1904–1984).

From here, make your way to Vermont Avenue NW, turn right, head toward T Street NW, and then turn left. The corner of T and 9th Streets NW is the site of the ⓫ WASHINGTON CONSERVATORY OF MUSIC AND SCHOOL OF EXPRESSION. Founded in 1903, it was one of DC's earliest Black institutions promoting the arts for children and adults. As a teenager, Ellington started to gain a reputation playing for society parties and felt the need for more formal training. According to his biography, he "jumped at the opportunity" to be taught by Henry Grant, his high school music teacher and one of the first graduates of the Conservatory, who taught "most of the advanced musicians."

Popular Nellie's Sports Bar, at 9th and U Streets NW, stands where ⓬ ADDISON SCURLOCK PHOTOGRAPHY STUDIO once thrived. Addison Scurlock (1883–1964) was one of the first photographers to chronicle the lives of Black people with dignity and sophisti-

cation. Having one's picture in Scurlock's studio was a mark of social status, and no Black dignitary's visit to DC was complete without a Scurlock sitting. Ellington was among many Black celebrities to receive the Scurlock treatment, along with the likes of W.E.B. Du Bois (1868–1963) and Booker T. Washington (1856–1915). Thousands of Scurlock's photographs have been donated to the Smithsonian Institution.

Continue walking on U Street NW, which merges with Florida Avenue NW. When you reach 7th Street NW, turn right, then make a left on T Street NW. While the Duke took music lessons and played gigs around Shaw, it was at ⑬ **FRANK HOLLIDAY'S POOL ROOM** in the early 1900s, which is **RIGHT PROPER BREWING COMPANY** today, that he developed his musical sensibilities. Ellington credited his time hanging out at Holliday's for helping shape his musical style. The back wall inside and to the right is the only remaining part of the original pool hall. It is decorated with a mural titled *Homage to Duke Ellington*.

New York had the Apollo Theater. Washington, DC had ⑭ **THE HOWARD THEATRE.** Next door to Holliday's, the legendary theatre was built in 1910, predating the Apollo by several years and achieving fame far earlier. It played host to many of the great Black musical artists of the early and mid-20th century, such as Ella Fitzgerald, The Supremes, Stevie Wonder, Marvin Gaye, and Chuck Brown. When the Howard reopened after renovations in 1931, Ellington was its first performer. Icons who performed here are commemorated on the Howard Walk of Fame, DC's version of the Hollywood Walk of Fame.

In front of The Shaw apartment building is ⑮ **ENCORE, A SCULPTURE OF DUKE ELLINGTON.** It depicts him sitting on a fanciful treble clef sign and playing a tune on a piano. The notes wrap around him and spiral upward, carrying his music and legend beyond his hometown and into history. Duke Ellington's legacy in Shaw endures through its lasting impact on jazz and the community's cultural vibrancy.

Opposite: The Howard Theatre

SHAW & GREATER U STREET NW

1 THURGOOD MARSHALL CENTER FOR SERVICE AND HERITAGE
1816 12th Street NW
Washington, DC 20009
www.tmcsh.org

2 DUKE ELLINGTON RESIDENCES #1 AND #2
1805 13th Street NW & 1816 13th Street NW
Washington, DC 20009

3 WHITELAW HOTEL (NOW WHITELAW APARTMENTS)
1839 13th Street NW
Washington, DC 20009

4 LINCOLN THEATRE
1215 U Street NW
Washington, DC 20009
www.thelincolndc.com

5 NEGRO LEAGUE BASEBALL MURAL
Lincoln Theatre alleyway
1215 U Street NW
Washington, DC 20009

6 BEN'S CHILI BOWL
1213 U Street NW
Washington, DC 20009
www.benschilibowl.com

7 TRUE REFORMERS BUILDING
1200 U Street NW
Washington, DC 20009
www.publicwelfare.org/true-reformer-building

8 INDUSTRIAL BANK OF WASHINGTON
2000 11th Street NW
Washington, DC 20001
www.industrial-bank.com

9 BOHEMIAN CAVERNS
2001 11th Street NW
Washington, DC 20001

Left: African American Civil War Memorial

10 PRINCE HALL MASONIC TEMPLE
1000 U Street NW
Washington, DC 20001
www.mwphgldc.com

11 WASHINGTON CONSERVATORY OF MUSIC AND SCHOOL OF EXPRESSION
902 T Street NW
Washington, DC 20001

12 ADDISON SCURLOCK PHOTOGRAPHY STUDIO
Nellie's Sports Club
900 U Street NW
Washington, DC 20001

13 FRANK HOLLIDAY'S POOL ROOM/RIGHT PROPER BREWING COMPANY
624 T Street NW
Washington, DC 20001
www.rightproperbrewing.com

14 HOWARD THEATRE
620 T Street NW
Washington, DC 20001
www.thehowardtheatre.com

15 *ENCORE*, DUKE ELLINGTON STATUE
618 T Street NW
Washington, DC 20001

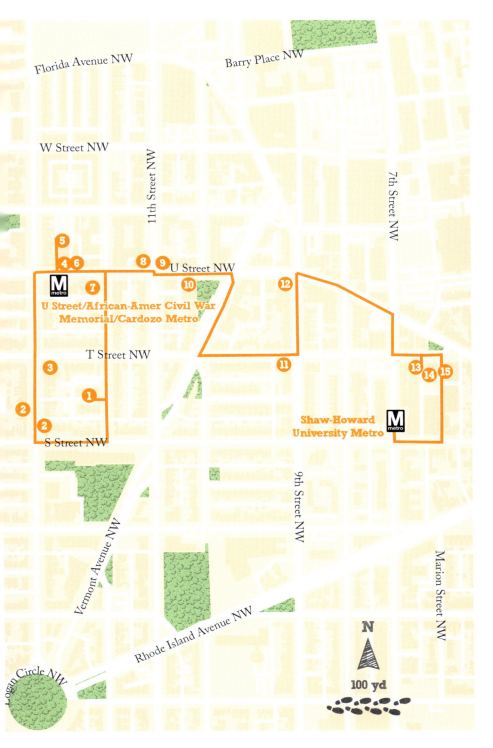

3 Art Deco Walk

Stories of beautiful buildings and their residents

> **BEST TIME:** Any season or time of day
> **DISTANCE:** Approximately 1 mile
> **ROUTE DESCRIPTION:** Easy walk, gentle uphill grade
> **START:** Metro at Woodley Park-Zoo/Adams Morgan (Red Line)
> **END:** Metro at Van Ness (Red Line)

When you think of architecture in Washington, DC, you may conjure up visions of neoclassical structures, brutalist buildings, or generic office buildings. But during the 1930s, Art Deco began making an appearance, balancing opulence and practicality. It influenced fashion, art, homeware, and building styles in the US and Europe throughout the Roaring Twenties and the Great Depression. Examples of Art Deco are scattered around the District. Over 400 Art Deco structures were constructed in the nation's capital until the 1940s, but many have been demolished or remodeled.

The greatest cluster of Art Deco buildings is located along Connecticut Avenue in Cleveland Park. Named for President Grover Cleveland (1837–1908), the suburb was once promoted as "the queen of the Washington neighborhoods." According to Steve Knight, President of the Art Deco Society of Washington, this stretch of road was the equivalent of Michigan Avenue in Chicago or Park Avenue in New York in terms of its prestige during its heyday.

While this walk will primarily focus on Art Deco buildings, you'll see other styles to illustrate Cleveland Park's architectural diversity, as well as landmarks that are significant in the neighborhood's history.

❶ **THE PARKWEST** is a prime example of Streamline Moderne, a style of Art Deco design that emerged in the 1930s. The building's architects Charles Dillon and Joseph Abel of the firm Dillon & Abel

Opposite: The Parkwest apartment building

Above: The iconic Kennedy-Warren apartment building
Left: Yenching Palace Right: Connecticut Avenue Bridge

were the first to introduce the style to DC in 1936. Continuing on Connecticut Avenue NW, you'll come to the ❷ KENNEDY-WARREN on the right, which is considered the largest and best example of Art Deco in the District. Architect Joseph Younger (1894–1932) designed the residential building in 1932 to have 441 luxury apartments with 2,029 total rooms at an estimated cost of $3,200,000 ($65,000,000 in today's value). But financing fell through due to the Great Depression, and the builders declared bankruptcy with only half of the original design completed. It took 70 years, but the building was finally completed in 2002!

The Kennedy-Warren was the first building in DC to use aluminum extensively. The building's famed exterior includes Aztec eagles carved into limestone and vast use of aluminum decorations on the façade and in the marquee entrance, very unique for design-conservative DC. The luxury complex featured amenities such as a gymnasium, barber shop, beauty salon, small grocery store, billiard room, dining room, ballroom, and valet service. It even has its own private bar! The list of notable tenants have included Lyndon and Lady Bird Johnson when he was just a Texas Congressman, Hillary Clinton, baseball player Frank Robinson, writer P.J. O'Rourke, and many politicians and diplomats.

Steps away, the ❸ CONNECTICUT AVENUE BRIDGE is an Art Deco, steel-arch bridge that connects Cleveland Park and Woodley Park neighborhoods. By the 1930s, Connecticut Avenue had become a major thoroughfare, and automobiles had almost completely replaced horse-drawn vehicles. This bridge was built to provide a wider crossing that would safely carry pedestrians, cars, trucks, and buses, as well as streetcars.

Engineer Ralph Modjeski (1861–1940) and architect Paul Phillipe Cret (1876–1945) designed the bridge to be practical yet sophisticated and subtle, so as to not detract from the beautiful, wooded Klingle Valley that surrounds it. Look for the Art Deco chevron patterns on the railings and the eight lanterns on stone pedestals as you make your way to the other side of this historic bridge.

Further up Connecticut Avenue, you'll come to the historic ④ **UPTOWN THEATRE.** It opened on October 29, 1936 showing *Cain and Mabel,* a musical starring Clark Gable and Marion Davies, on its enormous, 40-foot-high, 70-foot-wide, curved screen. This movie palace was part of a trend in which shopping and entertainment moved away from downtown areas and into suburban ones. The single-screen movie theater was designed by John Jacob Zink (1886–1952), an architect whose firm designed over 200 theaters in the United States, including some 30 in the Baltimore-Washington region. Though it's currently closed, the Uptown's façade remains a notable example of Art Deco. The etched glass windows, neon sign, and the marquee with its streamlined silver aluminum bands and contrasting red bands put it clearly in the mainstream of Art Deco movie-house design of the '20s and '30s.

The Uptown hosted world premieres of several films, including *2001: A Space Odyssey* (1968), and *Jurassic Park* (1993). It was also among only 32 theaters nationwide to screen *Star Wars* in 1977.

Keep walking to ⑤ **SAM'S PARK & SHOP** by the Cleveland Park Metro station. While it looks like an ordinary strip mall, this structure changed how Washingtonians shopped in 1931. The idea that you could pull off the road, park your car, and get all your shopping done in one place was a game-changing innovation. It was recognized as the first shopping center in DC and one of the first in the region.

Located next to the firehouse is the former ⑥ **YENCHING PALACE.** It was a landmark in the 1960s and '70s, where diplomats and movie stars dined, secrets were told, and international crises were mediated. The building was restored to its 1945 appearance, retaining its diamond windows and Carrara glass Art Deco panels, when it went on to house a Walgreens, which is also now closed.

According to local lore, emissaries for President John F. Kennedy and Soviet leader Nikita Khrushchev (1894–1971) met at Yenching Palace to negotiate during the Cuban Missile Crisis. Legend has it they ham-

Opposite: The former Uptown Theatre

Above: Sedgwick Gardens building designed in 1931
Below: Architecture in Cleveland Park, a charming blend of styles

mered out the final details in one of the booths and avoided a war. In keeping with its Cold War legacy, there were rumors that at least one of its booths was fitted with secret listening devices, although which side was supposedly doing the listening remains a mystery. A press conference was held here to announce the arrival of two giant pandas gifted to the National Zoo in 1972 to symbolize the new openness between the US and China.

After a short walk, you'll come to **❼ THE BROADMOOR** on your right, another example of the grand, luxurious buildings that defined Cleveland Park. Opened in 1929, it was named after the hotel of the same name in Colorado Springs, Colorado. With eight stories, it is the tallest of the apartment buildings in Cleveland Park and was built with many features typical of a hotel at that time, including a large dining room, hairdresser, barber shop, and pastry shop, which gave it the ambience of a self-contained resort. Among notable residents were Congressman and Mrs. Richard Nixon, and Richard Todd Lincoln Beckwith, the last living descendant of President Lincoln.

Next, located at the corner of Connecticut Avenue and Sedgwick Street NW is **❽ SEDGWICK GARDENS.** Combining Art Deco motifs with Byzantine and Moorish influence, the building is a transition from the medieval revival styles of the 1920s to the more strictly Art Deco buildings of the 1930s represented by the Uptown Theater. The building was designed by prominent local architect Mihran Mesrobian (1889–1975) in 1931 for $500,000 ($10,000,000 in today's value), and opened in 1932. Its ornate decorations are a cornucopia of Art Deco style, with an entrance designed to draw the eye upward. The original wrought iron, Gothic style letters and numbers that spell out "3726 Sedgwick Gardens" are affixed to the front columns. All of Sedgwick Gardens' 116 units feature sun porches and bay windows, and larger apartments even included two bathrooms, considered an incredible luxury in the 1930s.

Here in Cleveland Park, Art Deco facades are a visual symphony of geometric patterns, bold lines, and vibrant colors that seamlessly melds history with the promise of the future. Each building tells a story, reflecting the craftsmanship and artistic innovation of a bygone era, while also embracing contemporary touches that speak to modern sophistication. These buildings capture the essence of timeless elegance, inviting residents and visitors alike to revel in the neighborhood's unique blend of historical significance and forward-looking spirit. Here, every corner whispers tales of the past and hints at the possibilities of tomorrow.

The Art Deco Society of Washington offers more ways to learn about Art Deco in the District. The organization is dedicated to the preservation of the architectural, industrial, decorative, and cultural arts of the Art Deco era. You can meet other local lovers of Art Deco at the society's tours and special events.

Left: Sam's Park & Shop sign

❶ THE PARKWEST
2929 Connecticut Avenue NW
Washington, DC 20008
www.pwestapts.com

❷ THE KENNEDY-WARREN
3131–3133 Connecticut Avenue NW
Washington, DC 20008
www.kennedywarren.com

❸ CONNECTICUT AVENUE BRIDGE
Connecticut Avenue
& Macomb Street NW
Washington, DC 20008

❹ UPTOWN THEATER
3426 Connecticut Avenue NW
Washington, DC 20008

❺ SAM'S PARK & SHOP
3505 Connecticut Avenue NW
Washington, DC 20008

❻ YENCHING PALACE
3524 Connecticut Avenue NW
Washington, DC 20008

❼ THE BROADMOOR
3601 Connecticut Avenue NW
Washington, DC 20008
www.broadmoordc.com

❽ SEDGWICK GARDENS
3726 Connecticut Avenue NW
Washington, DC 20008
www.sedgwickgardensapts.com

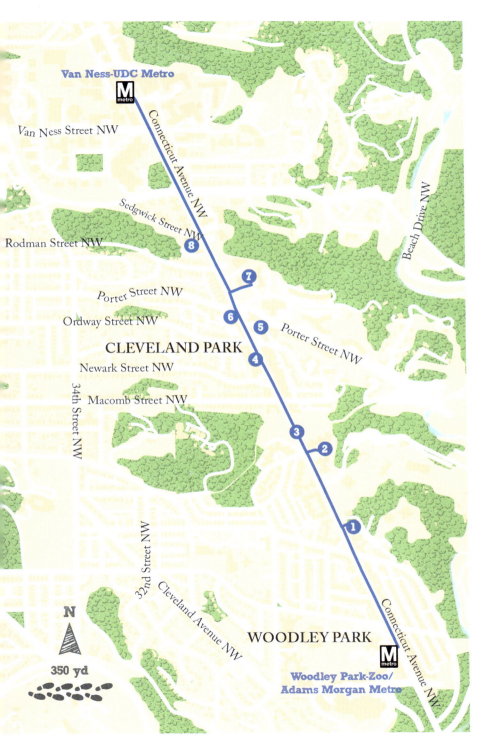

4 — Avenue of the Presidents Walk

Diplomatic & cultural spots with a bit of scandal

BEST TIME: Any season or time of day
DISTANCE: 1.3 miles
ROUTE DESCRIPTION: Moderate uphill grade
START: Metro at Dupont Circle (Red Line) or McPherson Square (Blue, Orange, Silver Lines)
END: Metro at Columbia Heights (Green Line)

On the city grid's north axis radiating from the White House, 16th Street is a notable thoroughfare. It has expanded from the President's neighborhood to the border with Maryland, replete with grand, historic churches, embassies, hotels, associations, and residences.

This street was part of the L'Enfant Plan for the city and evolved through the advent of the trolley lines during the Gilded Age just a few years after the Civil War. Expansion has continued with gentrification over time. The thoroughfare hosts a vast array of architectural styles that represent a who's who of noted architects of the late 19th and early 20th centuries. It is also sarcastically called "The Road to Heaven" for the more than 50 houses of worship from the White House to the Maryland border.

Begin at the newly reconstructed ❶ **EMBASSY OF AUSTRALIA**, described by its architects as a "monolithic form inspired by Australia's iconic landscape." Take note of the evocation of the Eucalypt forest, a diverse and unique ecosystem found in all Australian states and territories, depicted here in the exterior profile. The windows are meant to be an "urban room," reflecting the surrounding landscape.

Turn left on 16th Street NW. Up the block on the right is the ❷ **EMBASSY OF SERBIA**, the Italianate mansion built for Re-

Opposite: The venerable Chastleton Apartment

presentative George M. Robeson, who, as Secretary of the Navy under President Ulysses S. Grant, was instrumental in overseeing and developing early submarine and torpedo technology. The mansion has served as several diplomatic outposts and associations since 1881.

Two blocks up, the welcoming ❸ **FOUNDRY UNITED METHODIST CHURCH**, originally located on 14th Street, was built by Henry Foxall as a personal gesture of gratitude that his Georgetown foundry was spared from the fires set by the British in the War of 1812. Rebuilt in this location in 1903, the church regularly hosted Presidents Hayes and Clinton. The cornerstone was laid in a Masonic ceremony in which the gavel used was the same one with which George Washington laid the cornerstone of the US Capitol.

On the next block, the ❹ *ELLA THE ELEPHANT* SCULPTURE is at home on the grounds of the People for the Ethical Treatment of Animals (PETA) office. Retired from the circus and a pen pal to children inquiring about the life of elephants in captivity and the wild, she loves to read her favorite book, *Horton Hears a Who*.

Cross 16th Street NW to see the ❺ **EDLAVITCH DC JEWISH COMMUNITY CENTER (DCJCC)**. It opened in 1911 as the Young Men's Hebrew Association, formed by a group of Eastern European Jewish immigrants. Relocated to this location in 1926, it has expanded to become a center of culture, education, art, social justice, and sports. Notably, it is the home of Theater J, a multiple award-winning, professional company. Showcasing the richness of Jewish and global culture, history, and humor, the theater is fearless in its delivery of its diverse repertoire. Built in 1878, the photogenic ❻ **HUNTLEY HOUSE** stands directly across Q Street. Its rear carriage house, now a residence, remains one of the oldest in the city. Up the block is the ❼ **CHURCH OF THE HOLY CITY**, the first national church in DC, built in 1896. Look up at the stunning Tiffany windows.

A block up on the right, the ❽ **CHASTLETON APARTMENTS** is a breathtaking ode to Gothic Revival and whimsical gargoyles and spires. In 1919, it was the largest apartment building in DC, and quite swanky. General Douglas McArthur housed his mist-

Clockwise from top left: *Ella the Elephant;* Church of the Holy City; *Make Way for Ducklings;* DCJCC; Huntley House; Embassy of Australia

Above: Scottish Rite House of the Temple **Below:** Camden Roosevelt Building

ress there – legend has it that he snuck in to see her via a back stairway. If walls could talk!

Continue on for one block until you reach the ❾ **SCOTTISH RITE HOUSE OF THE TEMPLE.** The builders got special dispensation to install railroad tracks to transport its giant columns from Union Station to the site, and again to entomb two of its Grand Commanders above ground. James Smithson is the only other person with such privilege. John Russell Pope's design is based on the Tomb of Mausolus at Halicarnassus in Turkey, one of the Seven Wonders of the Ancient World. It boasts the first lending library in DC and offers tours of the extravagant interior loaded with Masonic symbolism.

Look left across 16th Street towards the French Renaissance-style mansion built originally for Supreme Court Justice Henry Brown, who authored the 1896 Plessy v. Ferguson decision that upheld racial segregation. In an interesting twist of fate, the ❿ **EMBASSY OF CONGO** now owns the building.

Turn right on S Street NW to where a neighbor installed a replica of the beloved Boston sculpture of ⓫ *MAKE WAY FOR DUCKLINGS* by artist Nancy Schön, and based on the classic children's book by Robert McCloskey. Now you can double back, turn right on 16th Street, and walk up five blocks.

Built in 1920, the ⓬ **CAMDEN ROOSEVELT BUILDING** was another one of the large residences that changed the face of 16th Street and made way for more up-and-comers to reside here. It became the elegant Roosevelt Hotel, and its popular Victory Room nightclub opened a month after the attack on Pearl Harbor. Greats like Benny Goodman, Glenn Miller, and Nat King Cole played there regularly, and live radio broadcasts from the club reached a national audience. After serving as a retirement community, the building was recently reverted back to apartments.

Look diagonally across the street at the red sandstone retaining wall that is ⓭ **A REMNANT OF HENDERSON CASTLE** that once stood above it, home to the inimitable Mary Foote Henderson (1832–1941) and her senator husband John (1826–1913). During his one term as a senator from Missouri, John co-sponsored the 13th Amendment to the US Constitution that abolished slavery. They returned home, where he earned great wealth, and she founded the St Louis School of Design. Upon their return to DC years later, Mary, a proponent of the City Beautiful Movement, made it her mission to establish 16th Street as the Avenue of Presidents, Embassy Row, and the ideal hillside for a new, larger White House. She planned on building a Lincoln Memorial across from her castle just above the former northern line of the city. The couple built several mansions that they rented or sold to be used as embassies and homes for the new wealthy. Her completed vision never came to life.

Continue across W Street NW and take any entrance to ⓴ **MERIDIAN HILL PARK**, dubbed Malcolm X Park by activist Angela Davis during a protest against police brutality in 1969. The land had been a Civil War encampment, and then it was a shanty town for freed African Americans until Mary Henderson procured it so that Congress could buy it and displace its many residents. The most magnificent feature here is the 13-tier fountain, the longest in the US, that cascades from the high point of the park. Look for the statue of Joan of Arc just above the fountain, the only female equestrian statue in the city. Newcomers are welcome to join the Sunday drum circle, ongoing since the week of Malcolm X's assassination in 1965. Originally about Black cultural awareness, the circle is now a happening that hosts musicians and audiences from the world over.

Use any of the park's exits and turn right, back onto 16th Street. Cross diagonally at Euclid Street, the stunning mansion of the ⓯ **INTER-AMERICAN DEFENSE BOARD**, once affectionately called the Pink Palace when Delia Field (1853–1937), widow of department store mogul Marshall Field (1834–1906), was in residence and had it painted, what else? Pink!

Two doors up from the formerly pink mansion is the upstairs Hemingway Bar (sadly not open to the public) at the on-again/off-again ⓰ **CUBAN EMBASSY**. The embassy has allegedly served up some "Daiquiri Diplomacy" over the years, and it reopened in 2015 after

Above: Embassy of Spain Cultural Center Below left: Musician & Polish Prime Minister Ignacy Jan Paderewski at the Embassy of Poland Below right: Inter-American Defense Board, or, The Pink Palace

decades of diplomatic surrogacy by Switzerland and Czechoslovakia. The mansion was built two decades after Cuba's independence from Spain, and in its time, it has been besieged and hit by Molotov cocktails a number of times in protest of the Castro regime and embargos, and yet it still stands in defiance.

Look across the street, the ⑰ **WARDER MANSION** has been saved twice from demolition and it was even moved 1.5 miles piece by piece to this location. It is the only remaining building in DC designed by Henry Hobson Richardson (1838–1886), who created it for Benjamin Warder (1824–1894), owner of one of the five farm machinery manufacturers that ultimately merged to become International Harvester.

Continue next door to the ⑱ **EMBASSY OF POLAND,** which uses its fence as an uncommon, frequently rotating, outdoor gallery to showcase art, photography, and historic events that celebrate this culture-rich nation.

Cross 16th Street at Fuller Street NW to the ⑲ **EMBASSY OF SPAIN CULTURAL CENTER,** housed in the ornate former residence of the Spanish Ambassador, designed by George Oakley Totten (1866–1939). Today, it hosts art, music, culinary, and other public events that celebrate Spain. You can even see art on the fence and installed in the windows.

Finally, walk next door and step inside the breathtaking ⑳ **MEXICAN CULTURAL INSTITUTE.** The recently restored, three-story mural here depicts the history of Mexico from the creation of Tenochtitlán to the annual Festival of Flowers. Renowned muralist Roberto Cuevas del Rio (1908–1988), a disciple of Diego Rivera, painted it over the course of eight years. See if you can spot Cuevas del Rio's self-portrait on the first floor. Spend a few moments in the exquisite, Talavera-tiled sunroom too. And be sure to come back for the regularly rotating exhibits in the galleries and the exuberant festivities and lectures.

Opposite: Joan of Arc statue in Meridian Hill Park

① EMBASSY OF AUSTRALIA
1601 Massachusetts Avenue NW
Washington, DC 20036
usa.embassy.gov.au

② EMBASSY OF SERBIA
1333 16th Street NW
Washington, DC 20036
www.washington.mfa.gov.rs

③ FOUNDRY UNITED METHODIST CHURCH
1500 16th Street NW
Washington, DC 20036
www.foundryumc.org/history

④ ELLA THE ELEPHANT
People for the Ethical Treatment of Animals (PETA) Office
1536 16th Street NW
Washington, DC 20005
www.petakids.com/meet-ella-elephant-wants-hear

⑤ EDLAVITCH DC JEWISH COMMUNITY CENTER
1529 16th Street NW
Washington, DC 20036
www.edcjcc.org

⑥ HUNTLEY HOUSE
1601 16th Street NW
Washington, DC 20036

⑦ CHURCH OF THE HOLY CITY
1611 16th Street NW
Washington, DC 20009
www.holycitydc.org

⑧ CHASTLETON APARTMENTS
1701 16th Street NW
Washington, DC 20009

⑨ SCOTTISH RITE HOUSE OF THE TEMPLE
1733 16th Street NW
Washington, DC 20009
www.scottishrite.org/our-museum

⑩ EMBASSY OF CONGO
1720 16th Street NW
Washington, DC 20009
www.ambadrcusa.org

⑪ *MAKE WAY FOR DUCKLINGS* SCULPTURE
1529 S Street NW
Washington, DC 20009

⑫ CAMDEN ROOSEVELT BUILDING
2101 16th Street NW
Washington, DC 20009

⑬ A REMNANT OF HENDERSON CASTLE
NW corner of 16th Street NW
at Florida Avenue NW
Washington, DC 20009

⑭ MERIDIAN HILL PARK OR MALCOLM X PARK
16th & W Streets NW
Washington, DC 20009
www.nps.gov/places/meridian-hill-park.htm

⑮ INTER-AMERICAN DEFENSE BOARD, AKA PINK PALACE
2600 16th Street NW
Washington, DC 20009
historicsites.dcpreservation.org/items/show/477

⑯ CUBAN EMBASSY
2630 16th Street NW
Washington, DC 20009
misiones.cubaminrex.cu/en/usa/embassy-cuba-usa

⑰ WARDER MANSION
2633 16th Street NW
Washington, DC 20009
www.wardermansiondc.com

⑱ EMBASSY OF POLAND
2640 16th Street NW
Washington, DC 20009
www.gov.pl/web/usa-en/embassy-washington

⑲ EMBASSY OF SPAIN CULTURAL CENTER
2801 16th Street NW
Washington, DC 20009
www.spainculture.us/city/washington-dc/

⑳ MEXICAN CULTURAL INSTITUTE
2829 16th Street NW
Washington, DC 20009
instituteofmexicodc.org

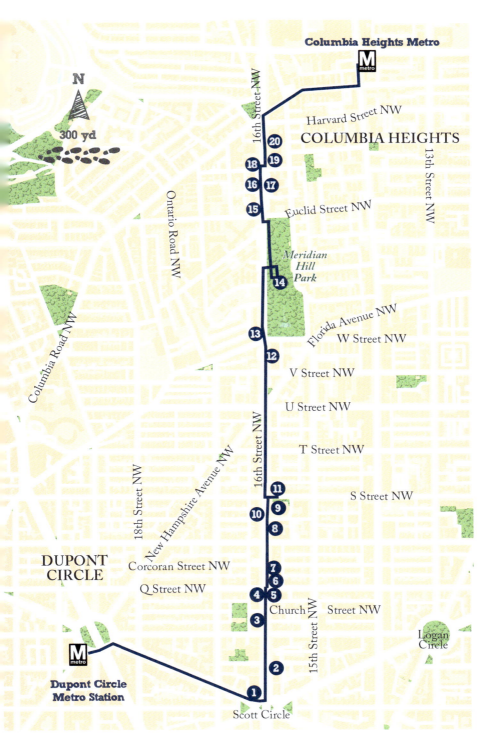

5 __ City Summit Walk

Ingenuity in the highest neighborhood in DC

BEST TIME: Any season or time of day
DISTANCE: Approximately 1.6 miles
ROUTE DESCRIPTION: Mostly flat with lots of visual stimulation for kids
START: Metro at Tenleytown-AU Station (Red Line)
END: Metro at Tenleytown-AU Station (Red Line)

Tennally Town, now Tenleytown, is the highest point in the city. It's named for John Tennally, who owned Tennally's Tavern, the first such establishment in Washington County, at what is now Wisconsin Avenue and River Road NW. The tavern served as a frequent stop for travelers and merchants. The second oldest neighborhood in DC may look quite residential, but it's actually replete with landmarked sites and it also has an ingenious side to it. That is the route you're embarking on now.

Down an alley off 45th Street and Burlington Place NW, you will find that upcycled plastics can be beautiful and clever, and they make a powerful social statement, too. One of the homeowners got the idea to decorate the fence on the alley side of her home and found herself creating a ❶ BOTTLE CAP MURAL. It looks like a series of kaleidoscopic postage stamps nodding to recycling, love, and Supreme Court Justice Ruth Bader Ginsburg (1933–2020). Bring your bottle caps to donate for future designs.

Head left on 44th Street and cross to see a funky ❷ WAYFINDING SIGN. It was a pandemic project to give neighbors a creative way of showing their love for their dogs, favorite vacation spots, and hometowns. You'll see a cacophony of color, style, and curiosity, and you'll want to spend a moment pondering the many beautiful ways people channel their affections.

Opposite: Former Perna Brothers Company

Just to the right, on Chesapeake Street, the ❸ NEON HOUSE was named by neighbors for the blazing neon sign made by one of the owners to indicate its street number. The house exudes childlike glee. There used to be a neon studio in the basement, but upon consideration, the artist owner decided that having a volatile gas and glass workshop in the house might not be wise. The regularly changed signs on the porch rail began as an ode to the names of local dogs, and then the owners started choosing their own words. It is now a destination for children to regularly get a new spelling word. Also enjoy the light art in the yard and a sparkling wave mosaic in the alley. If the owners are home, you might talk them into letting you choose the new word of the moment.

Continue three blocks on Chesapeake Street NW to the next alley and turn right. At the corner are samples of ❹ BRICK ROW HOUSES built by the Perna Brothers, immigrants from Italy who left their mark in residential stone masonry. Go down the alley to the photogenic black house, which was formerly the headquarters of the ❺ PERNA BROTHERS COMPANY, and read the plaque with the current owner's own sarcastic version of a historical marker.

Double back and cross Chesapeake Street NW to ❻ STEAK AND EGG DINER, a favorite neighborhood joint for nearly a century. It has cycled through a few franchise changes and remains a family-owned, independent, burger and all-day breakfast spot. Order a burger and strike up a conversation with Oz, one of the longtime cooks and an adventurous traveler.

Continue your walk by turning right out the door and walking one block on Wisconsin Avenue. Look just across the street, the Art Deco-style ❼ WESTERN UNION TOWER dominates the collection of TV and radio antennas, all strategically placed at the city's highpoint. In 1947, it was a great innovation in industrial engineering design and microwave radio technology for communications. Built to replace a wire telegraphy network, it was the first commercial network in the US to transmit and receive radio waves in a triangle that includes DC, Pittsburgh, and New York City.

Above: Perna Brothers brick row houses Below: Tenleytown Mural

Clockwise from top left: Tenleytown timeline inside the library; Western Union Tower; Residence of Japanese Ambassador; Neon House; Middle C Music; Wayfinding Sign

On the next block, step into the spirited ❽ MIDDLE C MUSIC, where even if you just want to browse, you might decide that it's finally time to take up that instrument you have always wanted to play. Not only is Middle C one of the coolest, lowest key music shops around, the owners also have sent instruments to the Landfill Harmonic orchestra in a Paraguayan slum, and they host music events for the neighborhood. The staff is always available to get you started on your musical journey. You can purchase an instrument, take music lessons, or buy sheet music and gifts.

Just across River Road NW, ❾ TARGET now occupies the 1941 Moderniste building that was originally a Sears & Roebuck. It was the first building to have a rooftop car park – and the rooftop snack bar was the hit of the neighborhood for years. Sears built it for retail expediency and introduced central heating and air conditioning, which was quite a treat for department store shoppers. Next came Hechinger's, the oversized hardware store, which served the neighborhood well until it sadly succumbed to competition.

Continue walking south on Wisconsin Avenue NW. On the second floor of the ❿ TENLEY-FRIENDSHIP LIBRARY, you'll find a photo-realistic timeline of the community expressed with images and the words of former residents. Take a few minutes to read the quotes to gain a deeper insight into the neighborhood. Across the avenue and down a block is the ⓫ TENLEYTOWN MURAL on the side of a nail salon. Painted by local artist Jarrett Ferrier, the mural pays tribute to places, people, and a Muppet. It is a fun spot to see if you can identify the stories depicted.

Go back across Wisconsin Avenue and fork left on Nebraska Avenue, passing American University's Washington College of Law, originally Immaculata Preparatory School for girls. Continue your walk for four blocks and cross Nebraska Avenue NW.

Pass the ⓬ NATIONAL PRESBYTERIAN CHURCH, which boasts an 86-bell carillon and 71 windows made by Willett, Tiffany, and Booth glass studios. The studios of ⓭ NBC4 TELEVISION STATION are located on the former site of the Naval Communications Annex and one of the outposts for the unsung Code Girls. They were thousands of young women recruited from elite universities who carried out top secret work during World War II. The women stationed here worked on deciphering code from intercepted communications transmitted by Bombe code-breaking machines, which ran 24/7 to simulate the rotors of the Enigma coding machines that transmitted messages from every German U-boat. The classified work at this location contributed to the breaking of the seemingly unbreakable Enigma Code, the Allied victory in the Atlantic, and the end of World War II. Local author Liz Mundy's book *Code Girls* is credited with piecing together the unknown stories of these remarkable women, including interviews with those still living a few years ago. Be sure to give a nod of thanks to these unknown heroines, who unknowingly aided the future of cyber security.

It is also in the NBC studios where college freshman Jim Henson (1936–1990) and his classmate Jane Nebel (1934–2013), whom he later married, made their first impression on the public in 1955. They introduced Kermit, who was not yet a frog, and their show quickly morphed into "Sam and Friends." Henson, Nebel, and their innovative team went on to create Kermit the Frog, Miss Piggy, Dr. Teeth and the Electric Mayhem, and their assemblage of Muppet friends who starred in television shows and movies. They also created subsequent animatronic and remote-controlled Muppets, whom you might spot if you look carefully at several Muppet movies and TV shows. These beloved creations endure to charm audiences and educate children across the globe.

Across the avenue is the ❹ **RESIDENCE OF THE JAPANESE AMBASSADOR** created by Japanese architect Isoya Yoshida (1894–1974), whose design reflects the harmony of one's life with nature. You can catch a glimpse of the grounds from the sidewalk, and the cherry blossoms here are radiant in springtime.

Head back along Nebraska Avenue and turn left on Warren Street. On the left, beyond the wall, is ❺ **DUNBLANE ESTATE,** the only known residence in DC designed by Gustav Stickley (1859–1942),

Above: Stickley–designed Dunblane estate
Below: Former Sears & Roebuck building, now Target

design innovator and the leader of the American Arts and Crafts Movement. The original owners of this 25-room mansion used a modified blueprint from a 1904 *Craftsman* magazine published by Stickley, and completed the home in 1911. It is one of the two remaining estates in Tenleytown.

❶ BOTTLE CAP MURAL
Alley behind 4437 Burlington Place NW
Washington, DC 20016

❷ WAYFINDING SIGN
NW Corner of 44th
& Chesapeake Streets NW
Washington, DC 20016

❸ NEON HOUSE
4335 Chesapeake Street NW
Washington, DC 20016

❹ BRICK ROW HOUSES
4112–4118 Chesapeake Street NW
Washington, DC 20016

❺ PERNA BROTHERS COMPANY
Rear alley behind
4615 42nd Street NW
Washington, DC 20016

❻ STEAK AND EGG DINER
4700 Wisconsin Avenue NW
Washington, DC 20016
www.steakneggdiner.com

❼ WESTERN UNION TOWER
Between 4621 & 4623 Wisconsin Avenue NW
Washington, DC 20016

❽ MIDDLE C MUSIC
4530 Wisconsin Avenue NW
Washington, DC 20016
www.middlecmusic.com

❾ TARGET, ORIGINALLY SEARS & ROEBUCK
4500 Wisconsin Avenue NW
Washington, DC 20016

❿ TENLEY-FRIENDSHIP LIBRARY
4450 Wisconsin Avenue NW
Washington, DC 20016
www.dclibrary.org/plan-visit/tenley-friendship-library

⓫ TENLEYTOWN MURAL
On the side of 4425 Wisconsin Avenue NW
Washington, DC 20016

⓬ NATIONAL PRESBYTERIAN CHURCH
4101 Nebraska Avenue NW
Washington, DC 20016
www.nationalpres.org

⓭ NBC4 TELEVISION STATION
4001 Nebraska Avenue NW
Washington, DC 20016
www.nbcwashington.com

⓮ RESIDENCE OF THE JAPANESE AMBASSADOR
4000 Nebraska Avenue NW
Washington, DC 20016

⓯ DUNBLANE ESTATE
4120 Warren Street NW
Washington, DC 20016

6 __ Creatives at Work Walk
Art, shops, and neighborhood vibes

> **BEST TIME:** Saturday mornings
> **DISTANCE:** Approximately 1 mile
> **ROUTE DESCRIPTION:** Easy, energizing, and colorful walk
> **START:** Metro at Brookland-CUA, CUA exit to left (Red Line)
> **END:** Metro at Brookland-CUA (Red Line)

Located in northeast DC, the Brookland neighborhood is known for two defining icons: the tower and dome façade of the Basilica of the National Shrine of the Immaculate Conception, and the bold, white "BROOKLAND" sign painted across nearly two stories of the Brookland Works building. Together, these two images represent the neighborhood's rich history and its recent developments.

Brookland was founded in the late 19th century. From 1801 to 1871, this area of DC was referred to as Washington County, and it was separate from Washington City and Georgetown. It began to take its form as a residential suburb in the 1880s, when Colonel Jehiel Brooks (1797–1886), for whom the neighborhood is named, sold nearly 150 acres of land, which was divided for the development of tracts of middle-class homes.

Over the years, Brookland has evolved into a diverse and vibrant neighborhood. The Roman Catholic Church built a lush campus for the Catholic University of America, and other religious institutions followed, earning the area the unofficial nickname "Little Rome." It has preserved much of its historical character while also welcoming new developments and a growing arts and cultural scene. The area along Monroe Street has reinvented Brookland as Washington's newest arts district.

On Saturdays, the Arts Walk plaza buzzes with people and pets going to the farmers market. You'll find a little bit of everything, like

Opposite: Pearl Bailey mural at Busboys & Poets in Brookland

Left: Transformation Junkies

fresh fruit and produce, kimchi and empanadas, hot coffee and tea, and even ice-cold beer. The year-round market occasionally hosts special events, including live music and yoga.

The ❶ **WALL OF THE BROOKLAND-CUA METRO STATION** to the left is dominated by a large-scale mural by DC artist Rajan Sedalia. The mural showcases elements such as books, musical instruments, religious symbolism, and people from different walks of life, celebrating the diversity and culture of the neighborhood.

Head toward the courtyard and the vertical "Arts Walk" sign. Arts Walk features more than 20 artist studios, galleries, and creative spaces, where you'll find artists creating work in a wide variety of media. Galleries line the brick-paved pedestrian promenade so you can see artists in action. Each studio has its own hours, but many are open Saturdays from 10am–4pm.

The ❷ **AMERICAN POETRY MUSEUM (APM),** located in the shadow of the "Art Walk" sign in Studio 25, is not a museum in the traditional sense. It's an "anti-museum" focused on making poetry more accessible. APM serves as a gathering space for Washington's "academic" and "street" poets and offers space for exhibitions and education centered on the subject of American poetry. Visitors are welcome to come in and work on their own poetry – there's an old typewriter just waiting to be used – and chat with any of the poets in attendance. There are regular exhibits of art by local artists, and open mic events on first Fridays feature musicians and poets performing together. APM is the kind of place former Brookland resident, poet, and Howard University professor Sterling A. Brown (1901–1989) would have frequented. A central figure in the New Negro Renaissance of the 1920s and 1930s, Brown was named the first Poet Laureate of the District of Columbia in 1984.

At ❸ **TRANSFORMATION JUNKIES** in Studio 8, you can "change the world one upcycled piece at a time." Tim Kime, owner and chief creative force, specializes in upcycling thrift buys and old items destined for the curb into one-of-a-kind treasures. Browse finished items that are for sale or commission a project. You can also learn to create your own masterpiece. The shop is on the corner on the opposite side of the walkway.

If you love vintage and nostalgic items, walk to ❹ **ANALOG** in Studio 5 to the right on the main drag. You'll find a collection of handmade, unique stationery and snarky art prints made from recycled paper goods. Owner Melissa Esposito's love for stationery began as a child when she'd play Post Office, making notes, envelopes, and stamps for family members to deliver to each other. These street-level studios offer a unique opportunity for you to connect with DC's local creatives and makers all in one place. As you continue to amble along the promenade, observe the creative process and feel free to start a conversation or two.

The ❺ **MONROE STREET BRIDGE** will be to your left as you approach Monroe Street NE. Since 1997, the Young Masters, a community-based, non-profit organization that empowers young artists, has used art to transform the community landmark into a living memorial. Students from local schools have painted stars for their loved ones, and Brookland's youngest residents have added their handprints to welcome visitors to the community.

Cross Monroe Street NE, continue along 8th Street NE. Edgewood Arts Center, on the left, provides space for DC's artistic community to create and exhibit their work, and also serves as rental space for performances and classes. With its floor-to-ceiling windows, you'll be able to catch a peek at a hip-hop dance class or the next big theatrical production. Ahead, the building with the colorful mosaic used to be a one-story warehouse where artists came to hone their craft for more than 20 years. It has been transformed into a four-story campus where they can create and live. ❻ **BROOKLAND ARTSPACE LOFTS** is among the first of its kind in the District with 39 subsidized apartments designed to do double duty as studios and homes. The mosaic tile installation decorating the outside of the building was done by community volunteers.

Adjacent to Artspace is the ❼ **8TH STREET ARTS PLAZA** where the asphalt has been turned into a public art area. Five local artists were commissioned to design artwork for it. See if you can spot the mosaic benches, colorful "light bright" screen, and metal creatures on the downspout. Take time to check out the 750-square foot garden of native plants that has replaced asphalt and trash cans. A walkway with pavers etched with quotes gently leads you to a decorated bench where you can sit and be inspired by the creative energy.

❽ **DANCE PLACE** has been the artsy anchor of Brookland for over 45 years. Artist Christopher Janney created the two-story tower of translucent glass called Touch My Building, which makes sounds when passersby touch it. Founded in 1978, the dance and performing arts company is a renowned center for contemporary dance. It's no exaggeration to say that the Washington area owes much of its active dance scene to the training and classes offered at Dance Place. It was an early home to tapper Savion Glover. And the first performance outside New York by Blue Man Group took place here back when the avant-garde troupe was taking the world by surprise. You can take classes six days a week and see a performance just about every weekend. So stop to see what's on the schedule and get your tickets before continuing your walk.

Double back on 8th Street NE and walk to Monroe Street NE. By now, you've probably worked up an appetite. Head left on Monroe Street to the corner with Michigan Avenue NE and enter ❾ **BUSBOYS AND POETS.** This bohemian mini chain has made it their mission to connect with the artistic community, so it's the perfect place to cap

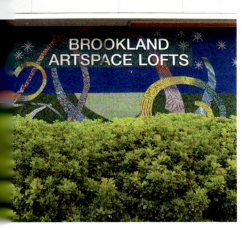
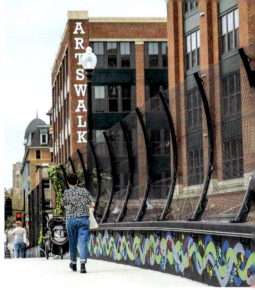

Clockwise from top left: Brookland Artspace Loft; Monroe Street Bridge; Poetry Museum; Rajan Selalia mural; Analog; Dance Place

off this artsy walk. The outdoor patio has a view of The Basilica of the National Shrine of the Immaculate Conception on Catholic University of America's campus, an area icon.

Busboys and Poets is a bookstore, restaurant, progressive event space, and a hub for writers, thinkers, and performers. Fittingly, it takes its name from the American poet Langston Hughes (1901–1967). Hughes worked as a busboy at DC's Wardman Park Hotel, where he became known as a "busboy poet" after his work was published. Inside, the Bailey Room event space is named after former Brookland resident and actress Pearl Bailey (1918–1990), and local art is featured throughout the restaurant to show its roots within the community.

Browse around the bookstore, which offers books by local authors. Try the Poet Mojito or the Hurston Cooler (named for poet Zora Neale Hurston), and let yourself be inspired by all the creativity around you.

❶ BROOKLAND-CUA METRO MURAL
Michigan Avenue NE entrance/exit of the Brookland-CUA Metro

❷ AMERICAN POETRY MUSEUM
716 Monroe Street NE
Studio 25
Washington, DC 20017
www.apoetmuseum.org

❸ TRANSFORMATION JUNKIES
716 Monroe Street NE
Studio 8
Washington, DC 20017
www.transformationjunkies.net

❹ ANALOG
716 Monroe Street NE
Studio 5
Washington, DC 20017
www.shopanalog.com

❺ MONROE STREET BRIDGE
Monroe Street NE
Washington, DC 20017

❻ BROOKLAND ARTSPACE LOFTS
3305 8th Street NE
Washington, DC 20017
www.artspace.org/brookland

❼ 8TH STREET ARTS PLAZA
Lot between Brookland Artspace Lofts (3305 8th Street NE Washington, DC 20017) and Dance Place (3225 8th Street NE, Washington, DC 20017)

❽ DANCE PLACE
3225 8th Street NE
Washington, DC 20017
www.danceplace.org

❾ BUSBOYS AND POETS
625 Monroe Street NE
Washington, DC 20017
www.busboysandpoets.com

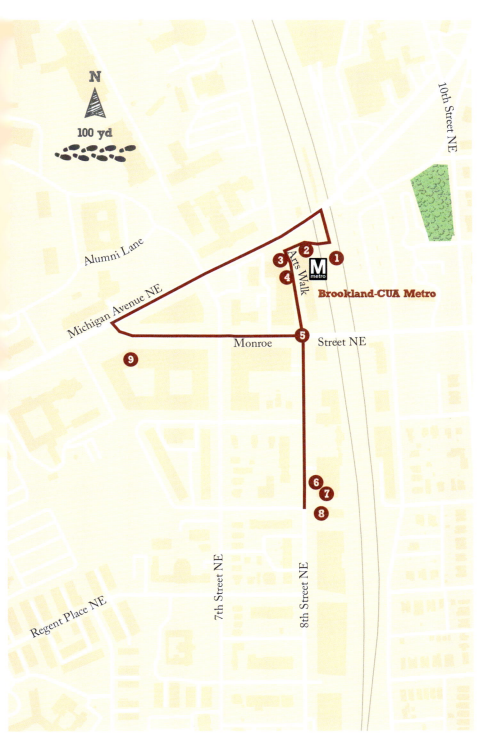

7 — Flags of Embassies Walk

International stories through the history of flags

> **BEST TIME:** Spring and fall on a windy day
> **DISTANCE:** 1.9 miles
> **ROUTE DESCRIPTION:** Gentle downhill grade, beautiful when flags are fluttering
> **START:** Metro at Tenleytown-AU (Red Line) to 31, 33, 96, N2 bus
> **END:** Metro at Dupont Circle (Red Line)

Of the 195 countries in the world, 177 host embassies and diplomatic missions in DC.

As you walk down Embassy Row, you'll begin to think about sites and the scenery of distant countries. Take some time to consider the colors and symbolism of the flags that fly in front of these sovereign tracts of foreign soil. Did you know that over 100 flags have stripes and bands of color? Over 30 flags use blue, white and red combinations. 64 flags contain religious symbols, and only 3 contain purple. Belize's flag has the most colors – 12. And Afghanistan's flag has been changed 30 times in 102 years. Many flags originated as maritime navigational emblems.

Begin your walk around the world at the ❶ **EMBASSY OF NEPAL**, whose flag is the only one that is neither rectangular nor square. The flag's two triangles represent the Himalayas and two religions, Hinduism and Buddhism. The blue represents peace, and red is the color of rhododendron, Nepal's national flower. The moon and sun originally represented the Rana dynasty, the totalitarian, self-proclaimed "prime ministers for life", with the desire that the country might live as long as these celestial bodies.

Walk left on 34th Place NW, turn left onto Massachusetts Avenue. What's commonly known as Embassy Row runs from this point to Dupont Circle.

Opposite: Embassy of Norway, one of the first to fly a flag in DC

Above: Brazil's "Order and Progress" Below: Cherry blossoms along Embassy Row

The blue, white, and red cross on the flag at the ❷ **ROYAL NORWEGIAN EMBASSY** was influenced by the French Tricolore, the renowned symbol of liberty from the 18th century, as well as the flags of the United States and United Kingdom, two other countries that were not ruled by an absolute monarch. The white cross on a red field is taken from the Danish. Established in 1905, Norway's was one of the earliest embassies in DC, representing one of the co-founders of both the United Nations and NATO.

Across 34th Street flies the flag of the ❸ **APOSTOLIC NUNCIATURE OF THE HOLY SEE,** or the Vatican, the smallest independent state in the world. It is located within Rome, and its authority is confined to Vatican City. Yellow and white representing gold and iron have been used since the Middle Ages on papal coats of arms. Here, they denote the colors of the keys to the Kingdom of Heaven that Christ bestowed upon Saint Peter. The emblem is that of the Vatican as headquarters of the Roman Catholic Church and has been in use since the 13th century. The triple crowns represent the three types of secular power – legislative, executive, and judicial – vested in the Pope, the successor to Saint Peter. Going back to the 4th century, the Vatican has the longest tradition of diplomatic relations of any sovereignty in the world.

Cross and continue down Massachusetts Avenue NW to the ❹ **BRITISH EMBASSY.** A jack, or a small flag, usually a square, was customarily hoisted from the jackstaff on the bow of a sailing ship in harbor. The Union Jack is the combination of crosses of the patron saints of England, Scotland, and Ireland: George, Andrew, and Patrick, respectively. The saltire, a motif based on Saint Andrew's cross, is a heraldic symbol said to have originated in battle during the Dark Ages. It is the oldest heraldic symbol in Europe. The UK built the first purpose-designed embassy in DC in 1872, which was demolished in 1931.

Across the avenue, the ❺ **EMBASSY OF SOUTH AFRICA** flies its flag of six colors. Created in 1994 after independence and the swearing-in of Nelson Mandela, the blue, white, and red elements stand for the Boer republics, and the black, green, and yellow for the African

National Congress. The Y-shape represents the transformed country's intersection and unification, or convergence rather than divergence, of the two separate paths of South Africans and its European colonizers. At the time of its adoption, it was the only flag of six colors.

Keep walking to the ❻ **EMBASSY OF THE PLURINATIONAL STATE OF BOLIVIA**, a country named for Simón Bolívar, who supervised its secession from Spain in 1825. This embassy flies an ornate flag with the dominant image of a powerful, courageous, and ever-watchful Andean Condor looking down over the nation and protecting it under the cover of its enormous spread wings, always at the ready to vanquish its enemies. Deference to the Inca culture is reflected in the yellow stripe.

Outside the black cube that is the ❼ **EMBASSY OF BRAZIL AND THE ADJACENT AMBASSADOR'S RESIDENCE**, "Order and Progress" is emblazoned on the banner that crosses the field of stars representing 26 states and the federal district. The constellation is Canis Major, which sparkled over Rio de Janeiro on November 15, 1889, the day the republic proclaimed its independence from Portugal.

The abandoned ❽ **FORMER EMBASSY OF IRAN** across the avenue has not flown its flag since 1979, when US relations were severed during the hostage crisis and the overthrow of the Shah. The building itself, along with the adjacent former residence of its ambassador, stand as remnants of an era of high politics, wild parties, and debauchery worthy of a nation that was flourishing in its heyday under the rule of Shah Mohammad Reza Pahlavi (1919–1980) and the stewardship in the US of debonair Ambassador Ardeshir Zahedi (1928–2021). Zahedi was known for lavish excesses, like serving kilos of caviar at every embassy party, pouring top-shelf liquor, which is haram, or forbidden, in Islam, and dating notables like journalist Sally Quinn, Elizabeth Taylor (he allegedly drank champagne from her shoe), and possibly Barbara Walters. After the revolution, at the direction of Ayatollah Khomeini, Embassy employees notoriously dumped $22,000 ($41,000 today) of liquor down the drain. The US Embassy in Tehran would be turned into The US Den of Espionage Museum.

Above: The Iranian flag last flew at this noteworthy diplomatic outpost in 1979.

Turn right up Whitehaven Street NW to the ❾ **EMBASSY OF SRI LANKA,** which also boasts an immensely symbolic flag. Count the turns of the Eightfold Path of Buddhism in the tail of the lion. The four leaves in the corners represent the tree under which Siddhartha sat when he achieved enlightenment and became the Buddha.

Further on, the very sociable ❿ **EMBASSY OF DENMARK** was built in 1960 as the first Modernist-style embassy in DC. It flies the Dannebrog, the oldest continuously used flag in the world, originating in 1219. The well-told legend has it that the blood-red flag with a white cross fell from heaven during the 1219 Battle of Lyndanisse, now Tallinn, Estonia, during the northern Crusades. King Valdemar's troops were on the verge of losing the battle to the pagan Estonians. The retreating Danes caught the flag, the sign they needed to persist towards victory. They counter-attacked, crying, "Forward to victory under the cross!"

71

Above: Belize boasts the most colorful flag in the world.
Below: The Dannebrog is the oldest continuously used national flag in the world.

Double back, passing the architecturally rich ⑪ **ITALIAN EMBASSY,** with its Tricolore, introduced in 1796, changed several times until this version was adopted in 1946 after the end of the monarchy and establishment of the Italian republic. Turn right on Massachusetts Avenue. Cross the bridge over Rock Creek Park and cross the avenue.

In 1944 the beloved former Turkish Ambassador Mehmet Münir Ertegün died. To the dismay of the Muslim community, there was nowhere in DC to perform the appropriate religious rituals for the man who had firmly established newly sovereign Turkey as a US ally. He had been the longstanding Dean of the Diplomatic Corps, and he contributed greatly to the local Muslim community. After the ambassador's body was sent to Turkey, the idea to build the ⑫ **ISLAMIC CENTER OF WASHINGTON** regained momentum, spearheaded by the Egyptian envoy and a Palestinian-American developer. They purchased the property near the world's many embassies to build a center of culture and religion.

Twenty-one Muslim nations put aside differences and consolidated ideas and skills for this unified project. Craftsmen from across the Muslim diaspora created the religious and decorative motifs and ornaments with authentic detail for a venue that would be as elegant and graceful as other notable mosques around the world. Countries gifted materials, ornamentation, and funds. The unique design has the façade in line with Massachusetts Avenue, and the interior prayer hall faces towards Mecca. Look for the flags of the 21 participating nations flying in front of the mosque.

Now continue your walk down the avenue. Thanks to the Godolphin Treaty of 1670, control of Belize bounced between Spain and England for generations. The flag flying over the ⑬ **EMBASSY OF BELIZE** is the most colorful one on earth. Boasting 12 colors, this flag represents one of the 14 English-speaking nations in all the Americas. It has every element of a flag, from motto to symbology, not the least of which is the color of the complexions of the men in the crest, who were modified to represent Belizean Mestizos and Afro Belizeans, the only humans depicted on any national flag. At midnight on September 20, 1981, the lights over the Government House in Belize City were extinguished, and when a floodlight lit the flagpole a few moments later, this new flag of the liberated state had replaced the Union Jack.

The familiar yin and yang on the flag of the ⑭ **EMBASSY OF THE REPUBLIC OF KOREA,** just across, evokes a balance of the universe with its opposite aspects, accompanied by the four kwai, or trigrams. Yin is the broken bars, and yang is the unbroken bars. These trigrams represent the elements earth, air, water, and fire; of heaven, moon, earth, and sun; of the four seasons; and of the four cardinal directions.

Just to the left, another embassy whose flag has not flown since tenuous relations have been tested is that of the ⑮ **EMBASSY OF THE BOLIVARIAN REPUBLIC OF VENEZUELA,** though its flag's creator is of note. In a 1785 conversation between Johann van Goethe and General Francisco Miranda, a revolutionary who swore that he would fight against the kingdom of Spain to gain independence for Hispanic America, Goethe told him "Your destiny is to create in your land a place where primary colors are not distorted." Goethe went on to regale Miranda with his ideas on the symbolism of color. In the mid-1780s, Miranda traveled the United States, studiously observing the struggles of stabilizing a new nation, the insights from which he combined with his knowledge of Spain to better envision democracy and sovereignty of the Hispanic nations of the Americas. He is credited with being the creator of the flag of Gran Colombia, later subdivided into Venezuela, Colombia, Ecuador, and Panama. Venezuela's current flag dates back to 1864 and was the inspiration for the flags of Columbia and Ecuador.

Next door, the ⑯ **EMBASSY OF THE MARSHALL ISLANDS,** represents the archipelago of more than 1,200 islands, that are among the furthest east of Micronesia. In 1979, when the nation became independent of post–World War II US trusteeship, the new flag was raised. The winner of a flag design competition was First Lady Emlain Kabua (1928–2023), wife of the first President Amata Kabua (1928–1996), and supposed artist, though no record of her

Above left: Balancing the universe at the Embassy of the Republic of Korea
Above right: Symbols of Enlightenment at the Sri Lankan embassy

actual work is evident. The parallel stripes represent the equator, which lies just below the islands. The increasing width of the lines implies the growth and vitality of the newly sovereign nation.

In the next block, the flag at the ⑰ **EMBASSY OF CROATIA,** a country with aspirations of sovereignty and allyship with the Russian Empire, was inspired by the colors of the Russian flag. It is one of the most colorful standards, with six colors. The checkers go back to 925 A.D. and symbolize the Kingdom of Croatia. They are incorporated with the red, white, and blue stripes of Croatia, Slavonia and Dalmatia, and the shields represent the provinces dating back to the 12th century. This modern standard was adopted in 1991 after the breakup of Yugoslavia.

Continue across Sheridan Circle on the left to find that the flag flying at the ⑱ **EMBASSY OF TURKMENISTAN** holds the ho-

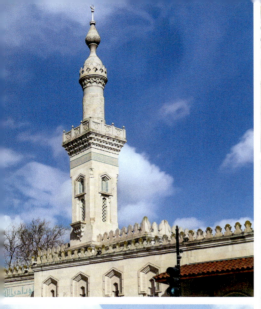

Clockwise from top left: Islamic Center of Washington; Ching Ching Cha Tea House; Kingdom of Morocco's Seal of Solomon; Great Britain's Union Jack

nor of being designated the most intricate national flag in the world – and with only four colors. With its rich, nomadic tradition of elaborate carpet weaving, five motifs of the five tribes run down the hoist. Five stars denote the nation's regions or tribes, the pillars of Islam, and the five senses. The five-pointed stars represent the states of matter – solid, liquid, gas, crystal, and plasma. Two gold olive branches were added later to denote neutrality in global relations.

At the end of the block on the right is the ⓲ **EMBASSY OF THE GRAND DUCHY OF LUXEMBOURG,** which had no flag at all until 1830, when patriots were encouraged to fly their colors, which evolved into the current tricolor. Look for the large plaque at the door that is a very public thank you to the American soldiers who liberated the Duchy during World War II.

Continue diagonally along Q Street, past the statue of Mahatma Gandhi, and turn left on 21st Street NW to the fitting last stop.

The flag that you'll see at the ❷⓿ **CONSULATE OF THE KINGDOM OF MOROCCO** was designed by the reigning Sultan Maulay Yusef ben Hassan in 1915, a red field with the green Seal of Solomon. After Morocco's independence from France in 1956, the flag remained as the national standard. In 1777, Sultan Mohammed III made Morocco one of the first countries to recognize the new United States by opening its shipping ports to American vessels. This relationship was solidified with a treaty of peace and friendship in 1786, making Morocco the 8th country to do so officially. Morocco remains the longest, unbroken foreign relationship for the US. In 1905, full diplomatic relations began between the two countries.

Even global citizens need a pick-me-up. So walk four blocks down 21st Street NW to ❷❶ **CHING CHING CHA TEA HOUSE** for a pot of tea served with all the traditions of China, Japan, Taiwan, and India. Every tea is served in its own unique vessel in accordance with the traditions of each type of tea and its origin.

❶ **EMBASSY OF NEPAL**
2730 34th Place NW
Washington, DC 20007
us.nepalembassy.gov.np

❷ **ROYAL NORWEGIAN EMBASSY**
2720 34th Street NW
Washington, DC 20008
www.norway.no/en/usa/norway-usa/about-embassy/

❸ **APOSTOLIC NUNCIATURE OF THE HOLY SEE**
3339 Massachusetts Avenue NW
Washington, DC 20008
www.nuntiususa.org

❹ **BRITISH EMBASSY**
3100 Massachusetts Avenue NW
Washington, DC 20008
www.gov.uk/world/organisations/british-embassy-washington

❺ EMBASSY OF SOUTH AFRICA
3051 Massachusetts Avenue NW
Washington, DC 20008
www.saembassy.org

❻ EMBASSY OF THE PLURI-NATIONAL STATE OF BOLIVIA
3014 Massachusetts Avenue NW
Washington, DC 20008

❼ EMBASSY OF BRAZIL
3006 Massachusetts Avenue NW
Washington, DC 20008
www.gov.br/mre/pt-br/embaixada-washington

❽ FORMER EMBASSY OF IRAN
3003 Massachusetts Avenue NW
Washington, DC 20008
www.boliviawdc.org/en-us

❾ EMBASSY OF SRI LANKA
3025 Whitehaven Street NW
Washington, DC 20008
slembassyusa.org

❿ EMBASSY OF DENMARK
3200 Whitehaven Street NW
Washington, DC 20008
usa.um.dk

⓫ ITALIAN EMBASSY
3000 Whitehaven Street NW
Washington, DC 20008
ambwashingtondc.esteri.it/en

⓬ ISLAMIC CENTER OF WASHINGTON DC
2551 Massachusetts Avenue NW
Washington, DC 20008
www.theislamiccenter.us

⓭ EMBASSY OF BELIZE
2535 Massachusetts Avenue NW
Washington, DC 20008
www.belizeembassyusa.mfa.gov.bz

⓮ EMBASSY OF THE REPUBLIC OF KOREA
2450 Massachusetts Avenue NW
Washington, DC 20008
overseas.mofa.go.kr/us-en/index.do

⓯ EMBASSY OF THE BOLIVARIAN REPUBLIC OF VENEZUELA
2443 Massachusetts Avenue NW
Washington, DC 20008
www.britannica.com/topic/flag-of-Venezuela

⓰ EMBASSY OF THE MARSHALL ISLANDS
2433 Massachusetts Avenue NW
Washington, DC 20008
rmiembassyus.comcastbiz.net/index.php

⓱ EMBASSY OF CROATIA
2343 Massachusetts Avenue NW
Washington, DC 20008
mvep.gov.hr/embassy-114969/contacts-and-working-hours-114970/114970

⓲ EMBASSY OF TURKMENISTAN
2207 Massachusetts Avenue NW
Washington, DC 20008
usa.tmembassy.gov.tm/en

⓳ EMBASSY OF THE GRAND DUCHY OF LUXEMBOURG
2200 Massachusetts Avenue NW
Washington, DC 20008
washington.mae.lu/en

⓴ CONSULATE OF THE KINGDOM OF MOROCCO
1601 21st Street NW
Washington, DC 20009
https://us.diplomatie.ma/en

㉑ CHING CHING CHA TEA HOUSE
1314 21st Street NW
Washington, DC 20036
www.chingchingcha.com

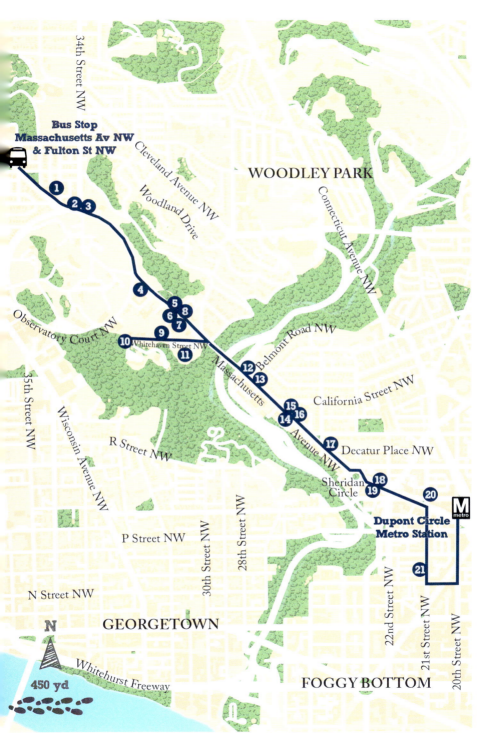

8 Food Lovers Walk
Tantalizing tour of culinary diversity

> **BEST TIME:** Weekend mornings
> **DISTANCE:** Approximately 1 mile
> **ROUTE DESCRIPTION:** Easy, flat terrain, and stroller-friendly
> **START:** Metro at NoMa-Gallaudet/New York Avenue (Red Line)
> **END:** Metro at NoMa-Gallaudet/New York Avenue (Red Line)

Union Market Terminal officially opened in February 1931. Savvy Washingtonians knew this was the place to come for the lowest prices, exotic foods, and other items that couldn't be found elsewhere in the city. Over the decades, however, the area fell into disrepair, and the Union Market building and many of the surrounding buildings were purchased in 2007 by EDENS, a national retail real estate developer. Re-opened in 2012, the Union Market area features more than 40 local food vendors.

Inside Union Market, you'll find a dizzying array of dining options in a chaotic maze of aisles. Head down the aisle to your right all the way to the end, take a left and go to the end of the aisle. ❶ **HARVEY'S MARKET** is a carnivore's dream. The legacy store has an established following that goes back generations. It first operated in 1931 at the O Street Market (no longer in existence) and has been at Union Market since 1971.

Two stalls down to the right, ❷ **ALMAALA FARMS,** also part of the old market, is known for their peaches, grapes, okra, and tomatoes. What can't be found at their stall can be supplemented at the Sunday farmers market at the Plaza at The Dock, adjacent to the market. Known for its "divine Southern-style comfort food," ❸ **PUDDIN'**, to the left, has been serving up bread pudding and gumbo since 2010. Don't leave without trying their signature dish (and the inspiration

Opposite: St. Anselm

Clockwise from top left: Bidwell restaurant; Harvey's Market; Capital Bikeshare; District Doughnuts

for the eatery's name): the Brown Butter Bourbon Bread Puddin'. They'll give you a sample if they're not too busy.

At the next aisle, turn left. Cooks and foodies go to ❹ CUCINA AL VOLO for their handmade, fresh, Bolognese-inspired pasta and sauces. Take home the lamb ragù or serve the spinach-and-ricotta ravioli at your next dinner party. Next, you'll travel from Italy to the Big Apple. ❺ BUFFALO AND BERGEN, on the right, is an unconventional cross between an old-school soda fountain, diner, bar, and Jewish deli, that specializes in handcrafted sodas, classic egg creams, and ice cream floats. Try a New York-style bagel sandwich or go for a bit of the "hair of the dog" with a towering "Lox'd & Loaded Bloody Mary," which is garnished with an everything bagel topped with lox, cream cheese, capers, and red onion.

❻ BIDWELL is the market's only sit-down restaurant and serves up Southern-inspired dishes. They take "farm-to-table" and top it – quite literally – by serving produce grown on a rooftop garden. The restaurant was named a Bib Gourmand honoree in DC's Michelin Guide. It's also worth noting that the cornflake-crusted French toast on the brunch menu is *chef's kiss*.

Take a moment to look up. The chandeliers overhead add a chic touch to the industrial space, but there is more to them than meets the eye. Those elegant light fixtures are actually made of upcycled water bottles. DC artist Dan Steinhilber uses everyday materials, so that most of his works can be recycled or reused. Check the Union Market's website for the rotating selection of pop-up artisans. You can expect something new with each visit.

Head outside and go left toward 6th Street NE. At the corner, turn left and look for the mural and the words painted on the wall. The market was home to a famous, desegregated boxing gym in 1949. Located above the market, the gym was owned by Billy Edwards, a 240-pound ex-fighter who was blind in one eye. He was nicknamed "Stillman of the South" after the legendary New York City boxer-trainer, and he trained about 75 fighters a day for $6 each. The gym's mascot, a wiry little terrier, was appropriately named Punchy.

Go around the next corner, and you'll find a mural that has received worldwide attention. Graffiti artist Mr. Brainwash spray-painted the words "Never Give Up" above a mass of colorful hearts in collaboration with former First Lady Michelle Obama in 2016 to celebrate International Women's Day.

Head to the end of the alley and turn right on 5th Street SE. ❼ COTTON & REED, to the left, has brought local rum into the forefront with its bespoke distillery and tasting room. Think farm-to-table but with rum. Opened in 2016, the distillery was created by two former NASA strategists, Reed Walker and Jordan Cotton, who share a common love for the spirit. There hasn't been local rum in the city limits since the Temperance League marched on Pennsylvania Avenue in 1913 and pronounced their opponents "rummies." Housed in a 90-year-old warehouse, the distillery offers tours on Saturdays.

Continue on, turn left on Penn Street NE, and follow Penn to 4th Street NE and make a left. At the upper end of the culinary scale is ❽ MASSERIA, hidden among the rows of wholesale stores. You might miss it if you don't know what you're looking for. But step inside the wooden gate that looks like a garden shed, and you're transported to Puglia and the heel of Italy's boot. It's become one of the in-places for in-the-know diners in DC, especially after it was awarded a Michelin star.

Walk to the corner of 4th Street and Neal Place NE. If the cornucopia of food at the market wasn't enough, more restaurants and bars can be found inside ❾ LA COSECHA, Union Market's Latin sibling. It is a mix of retail, restaurants, and bars from Latin American businesses and local Latin talents. At the center, Serenata, a pan-Latin cafe and bar, is ready to pour creative drinks. Helmed by Andra "AJ" Johnson, beverage director and co-founder of DMV Black Restaurant Week, it uses lesser-known spirits beyond mezcal. The mercado hosts a range of regular events, including salsa dancing lessons and empanada cooking classes. Their online calendar lists upcoming events.

Now go to Morse Street NE and turn left. At the Morse Street alley, turn left again. ❿ BREAD ALLEY comes by its name honestly: it sells bread and is literally located in an alley. It can be hard to find, so look for the words "bread alley" painted on the wall and follow the arrow. The diminutive shop recalls what it might have been like winding your way through bustling wholesalers in the early days of the

Opposite: La Cosecha, Union Market's Latin counterpart

Above: Michelin-rated Masseria restaurant **Below:** Almaala Farms

market. A favorite of local carb lovers, it features shelves of signature breads, like crusty French baguettes, as well as small-batch, local jams, butter, honey, and salts. Arrive early because they sell out quickly.

Back at the alley entrance, turn left. On the corner of Morse Street and 5th Street NE is ⑪ ST. ANSELM. Helmed by *Top Chef* alum Marjorie Meek-Bradley, the eatery has earned Michelin recognition for its unpretentious steaks and seafood. The buttermilk biscuits with pimento cheese alone are worthy of an award.

Cross 5th Street NE and look to the right for the green, white, and red Italian flag. ⑫ A. LITTERI has been the best Italian market and deli in the city for almost 100 years. From the outside, it doesn't look like much – blink and you'll miss it. Inside, however, the shelves are jam-packed with every type of pasta you can imagine, olive oil, tomato sauce, and a freezer full of freshly made lasagne and ravioli. The deli in the back is not to be missed. You'll find a colorful and flavorful array of cheeses, olives, meats, pizza, and best of all, homemade cannoli. Their sandwiches are regularly mentioned on local "best of" lists. You can order ahead or write out your request on one of the papers at the counter. A. Litteri is old-school, but they've been around for almost a century for a reason.

Double back to Morse Street NE and turn right. Sandwiched between a bookstore and a Japanese restaurant is ⑬ VILLAGE DC CAFE, the artsiest coffee shop and market in the area. Opened in 2019, it sources products from the Southeast and Northeast DC neighborhoods, boosting businesses that just don't get the kind of foot traffic that more touristy areas draw. It also hosts markets, concerts, and gallery nights.

In addition to all the restaurants, the Union Market area hosts around 300 community events a year, many of them free. Take advantage of the Sunday farmers markets, catch up with makers-in-residence, relax with views of the city at Hi-Lawn, or enjoy independent films at nearby Angelika Film Center Pop-Up.

Almost a century after it opened, Union Market continues to be a thriving food destination fulfilling Washingtonians' culinary cravings.

NORTH OF MASSACHUSETTS (NOMA) NE

1 HARVEY'S MARKET
1309 5th Street NE
(inside Union Market)
Washington, DC 20002
www.harveysmarketdc.com

2 ALMAALA FARMS
1309 5th Street NE
(inside Union Market)
Washington, DC 20002
www.unionmarketdc.com/
retailer/almaala-farms

3 PUDDIN'
1309 5th Street NE
(inside Union Market)
Washington, DC 20002
www.dcpuddin.com

4 CUCINA AL VOLO
1309 5th Street NE
(inside Union Market)
Washington, DC 20002
www.toscana-market.com/
cucina-al-volo

5 BUFFALO AND BERGEN
1309 5th Street NE
(inside Union Market)
Washington, DC 20002
www.buffalobergendc.com

6 BIDWELL
1309 5th Street NE
(inside Union Market)
Washington, DC 20002
www.bidwelldc.com

7 COTTON & REED
1330 5th Street NE
Washington, DC 20002
www.cottonandreed.com

8 MASSERIA
1340 4th Street NE
Washington, DC 20002
www.masseria-dc.com

9 LA COSECHA
1280 4th Street NE
Washington, DC 20002
www.unionmarketdc.com/la-cosecha

10 BREAD ALLEY
418 Morse Street NE
Washington, DC 20002
www.instagram.com/breadalleydc

11 ST. ANSELM
1250 5th Street NE
Washington, DC 20002
www.stanselmdc.com

12 A. LITTERI
517 Morse Street NE
Washington, DC 20002
www.alitteri.com

13 VILLAGE DC CAFE
1272 5th Street NE
Washington, DC 20002
www.facebook.com/thevillagecafedc

Below: DC is ranked among the greenest cities in the U.S.

ANACOSTIA, EAST OF THE RIVER, SE

9 Frederick Douglass Walk
Trace his impact and legacy through his footsteps

> **BEST TIME:** Anytime, best during spring, summer, and fall
> **DISTANCE:** Approximately 1 mile
> **ROUTE DESCRIPTION:** Mostly flat with moderate uphill grade in historic neighborhood
> **START:** Metro at Anacostia (Green Line) to 90 Bus Martin Luther King Jr. Avenue SE & Marion Barry Avenue SE
> **END:** 90 Bus ML King Jr. Avenue SE & Marion Barry Avenue SE) to Metro at Anacostia Station (Green Line)

Once a thriving settlement of the Nacotchtank people, a Native American Algonquian tribe, Anacostia was incorporated as Uniontown in the mid-1800s as a suburb of the District. Employees from the Navy Yard just across the 11th Street Bridge began to settle here, as did Anacostia's most famous resident, abolitionist Frederick Douglass (1818–1895).

The neighborhood got its start thanks to developer John Fox and his business partners, John W. Van Hook and John Dobler, who named it Uniontown after their company, Union Land Association. After the Civil War, new towns called Uniontown started cropping up all over. To ease the confusion, Congress changed the name of this location in 1886 to Anacostia, derived from a Native American word meaning "village trading center."

Starting at the corner of Good Hope Road (now Marion Barry Avenue SE) and Martin Luther King Jr. Avenue SE, look to the right. The ❶ **11TH STREET BRIDGE** looms large in the neighborhood's history, starting with one of the most infamous incidents in American history. After assassinating President Abraham Lincoln (1809–1865) at Ford's Theatre, John Wilkes Booth's escape route took him right through Anacostia by way of Good Hope Road. For

Opposite: Anacostia historic marker

Above: Iconic neon Anacostia sign **Below:** Union Temple Baptist Church

generations, conspiracy chatter lingered among residents about the neighborhood's connections to the killing.

The Martin Luther King Jr. Avenue SE thoroughfare is an old Native American path once known as Piscataway Road, after the dominant regional tribe in the 1700s. Good Hope Road is another major thoroughfare still traveled today. The origins of the name have been debated for years, but what is certain is that Frederick Douglass walked on this road for about 15 years before his death.

Across the street, the ❷ NEON ANACOSTIA SIGN marks the gateway into historic Anacostia. The landmark is older than the famed Big Chair (which you'll get to soon). Even though several businesses have occupied the building, it's simply known to locals as the "Anacostia building." This intersection was Anacostia's first commercial center. From here businesses spread east on Good Hope Road and south along Nichols Avenue (what now is Martin Luther King Jr. Avenue SE). Among the earliest establishments were Robert Martin's general store and post office, his Farmers' & Drovers' Hotel, David Haines' blacksmith and wheelwright shop, Duvall's Tavern, and George Pyle's grocery.

Now walk down Martin Luther King Jr. Avenue SE. The building to the left just past U Street SE served as home to Curtis Brothers, once a household name for furniture. Up the street is a humongous chair named, appropriately ❸ THE BIG CHAIR, built by the Curtis brothers in 1959. The brothers launched a promotion that immortalized them in Anacostia folklore. On August 13, 1960, amidst the summer's heat and humidity, 21-year-old Lynn Arnold began living atop the Big Chair in a 10-by-10 foot glass house complete with a balcony. Dubbed "Alice in the Looking Glass House," Arnold lived inside it for six weeks. The existing Big Chair is a replica.

Continue walking to W Street SE and turn left. Founded in 1969, ❹ UNION TEMPLE BAPTIST CHURCH on the right has been at the epicenter of social justice movements for years. President Nelson Mandela and Winnie Mandela spoke here on several occasions, and it has been the apex for significant movements in the city's history, including the political comeback of Mayor Marion Barry.

The church has received acclaim for its 30-by-19-foot mural depicting the Last Supper, featuring the image of a Black Christ and disciples depicted as prominent Black Americans, including Martin Luther King, Jr., Rosa Parks, and Malcolm X. It's the only one of its kind in the US.

Continue on W Street SE to find more detached, small-frame houses in this area than any other 19th-century subdivision in the District. They reflect the early history of the Anacostia community.

Past 14th Street SE to the right is the home of Anacostia's most famous resident. In 1877, abolitionist Frederick Douglass purchased ❺ CEDAR HILL. The house was built by John Van Hook, one of the original Uniontown developers. Douglass paid the equivalent of $175,000 in today's dollars, making it the most expensive house in the District at the time. Douglass spent the last years of his life in Anacostia, where he finished the last of his autobiographies, *Life and Times of Frederick Douglass*. Public tours of the house led by National Park Service Rangers are available with reservations online.

Double back to 14th Street SE and turn right. Across from V Street SE is the Old Market House Square, a marketplace that was laid out in 1913 at the center of the Uniontown subdivision. It looks much the same today as it did then. From this corner, turn left onto V Street SE. The church on the corner of 13th and V Streets represents the early history of religion in Anacostia. ❻ SAINT TERESA OF AVILA CATHOLIC CHURCH is the oldest Roman Catholic Church in DC east of the Anacostia River. It is called the "mother church" because many area congregations are its offshoots.

Turn right on 13th Street SE and head toward U Street SE. Turn right and walk to ❼ 1312 U STREET SE. This is the oldest surviving house within the original Uniontown subdivision. Built in the early 1870s, it dates back to Frederick Douglass' early morning walks through the neighborhood. This block also features the work of Lewis W. Giles, Sr. at 1222 U (1933) and 1218 U Street (1940). He was an influential Black architect in the early 1920s, who worked with Isaiah T. Hatton, another prominent Black architect, whose buildings still exist on U Street NW.

Clockwise from top left: Honfleur Gallery; Cedar Hill; Mahogany Books; oldest home in the original Uniontown subdivision; Elife restaurant; The Big Chair

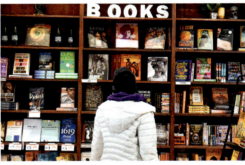

Head back to 13th Street SE and turn right. Continue to Good Hope Road SE and turn left. This corridor has been part of Anacostia's commercial center since the neighborhood was established. Today, it also comprises the Anacostia Arts and Culture District, a thriving creative hub.

❽ HONFLEUR GALLERY features contemporary art from national and local artists, including those from Anacostia. The gallery often hosts talks with the artists whose works are on exhibition here. ❾ KRAFT STUDIO next door is home to noted DC neon artist Craig Kraft. Look up at the Anacostia Arts Center sign to see an example of his work.

The ❿ ANACOSTIA ARTS CENTER is best described as an arts-focused mini-mall, with small stores, businesses, and galleries. The "W" in the tile at the main entrance serves as a reminder of its past life in the last century as a Woolworth. Inside is a rotating gallery of artwork by local artists and shops, including ⓫ MAHOGANY BOOKS, a Black-owned indie bookstore that specializes in books for, by, and about people of the African Diaspora. Located near the Big Chair, the Arts and Culture District includes the Anacostia Playhouse, which has built a reputation for presenting Helen Hayes Award-winning plays.

There are several places to dine in this area. ⓬ DCITY SMOKEHOUSE regularly tops "Best BBQ in DC" lists. At ⓭ OPEN CRUMB, next to Honfleur, the Opare family draws on their West African roots to create mouthwatering and affordable dishes. Plant lovers can savor vegan soul food at ⓮ ELIFE inside the Arts Center. Up the street is Southern Creole restaurant ⓯ KITCHEN SAVAGES. And ⓰ BUSBOYS AND POETS around the corner is a dining, bookshop, art gallery, and event space that feeds your mind, body, and soul.

Rich in local history, art, and culture, historic Anacostia retains a small-town feel and charm. And standing at the intersection of Martin Luther King Jr. Avenue SE and Marion Barry Avenue SE, Douglass' legacy of activism lives on.

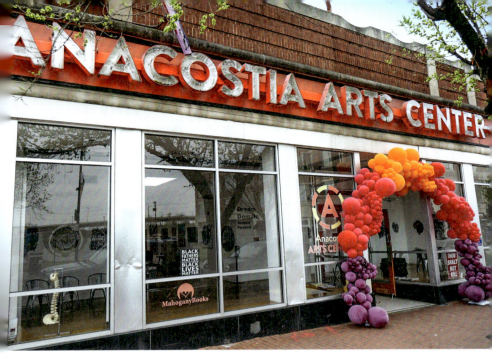

Above: Anacostia Arts Center
Below left: DCity Smokehouse Below right: Busboys & Poets

ANACOSTIA, EAST OF THE RIVER, SE

❶ 11TH STREET BRIDGE
Corner of Good Hope Road
& Martin Luther King Jr. Avenue SE
Washington, DC 20020

❷ NEON ANACOSTIA SIGN
Good Hope Road SE
& Martin Luther King Jr. Avenue SE
Washington, DC 20020

❸ THE BIG CHAIR
1001–1199 V Street SE
Washington, DC 20020

❹ UNION TEMPLE BAPTIST CHURCH
1225 W Street SE
Washington, DC 20020
www.uniontempledc.com

❺ CEDAR HILL
(Frederick Douglass Historic Home)
1411 W Street SE
Washington, DC 20020
www.nps.gov/frdo/index.htm

❻ SAINT TERESA OF AVILA CATHOLIC CHURCH
1244 V Street SE
Washington, DC 20020
Stachurchdc.org

❼ OLDEST HOME IN ANACOSTIA
1312 U Street SE
Washington, DC 20020

❽ HONFLEUR GALLERY
1241 Marion Barry Avenue SE
Washington, DC 20020
www.honfleurgallerydc.com

❾ KRAFT STUDIO
1239 Marion Barry Avenue SE
Washington, DC 20020
www.craigkraftstudio.com

❿ ANACOSTIA ARTS CENTER
1231 Marion Barry Avenue SE
Washington, DC 20020
anacostiaartscenter.com

⓫ MAHOGANY BOOKS
1231 Marion Barry Avenue SE
Washington, DC 20020
www.mahoganybooks.com

⓬ DCITY SMOKEHOUSE
1301 Marion Barry Avenue SE
Washington, DC 20020
www.dcitysmokehouse.com

⓭ OPEN CRUMB
1243 Marion Barry Avenue SE
Washington, DC 20020
www.opencrumbdc.com

⓮ ELIFE
1231 Marion Barry Avenue SE
Washington, DC 20020
www.eliferestaurant.com

⓯ KITCHEN SAVAGES
1211 Marion Barry Avenue SE
Washington, DC 20020

⓰ BUSBOYS AND POETS
2004 Martin Luther King Jr. Avenue SE
Washington, DC 20020
www.busboysandpoets.com

Left: Open Crumb African cuisine

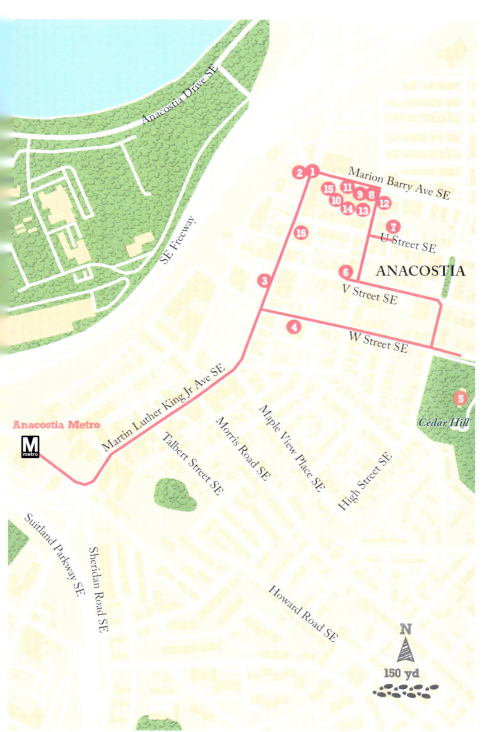

10 — Forgotten Georgetown Walk

Hidden history of a lost Black community

> **BEST TIME:** Best during spring, summer, and fall
> **DISTANCE:** Approximately 1.4 miles
> **ROUTE DESCRIPTION:** Mostly flat with a few hills along tree-lined streets
> **START:** G2 Bus to P Street NW & 27th Street NW
> **END:** Metro at Foggy Bottom-GWU (Blue, Orange, Silver Lines)

Many people are surprised when they learn that the chic Georgetown of today was once the center of transporting slaves from Africa to plantations in Maryland and Virginia. Georgetown was a separate entity adjacent to the District of Columbia, a bustling mix of white citizens and immigrants, and free and enslaved Black people. In the 1800 US Census, Georgetown had "1,449 slaves and 277 free blacks out of a total population of 5,120." It was an unusual dynamic, where enslaved and free Black people met and intermingled.

In the face of segregation, Black Georgetowners established a community that included a variety of clubs, sports teams, and Black-owned businesses. The 15-block area of Herring Hill gets its name from the fish peddlers who sold herring that ran in Rock Creek. Per the same Census, 851 families lived here. Many Black residents worked as gardeners and cooks for upper-class families, and some owned stores and barber shops. Herring Hill thrived well into the 1930s. The ❶ **HERRING HILL HISTORIC MARKER** at the intersection of P Street NW at 27th Street NW denotes the heart of this once thriving community. At the top of 27th Street is a path that leads to Mt. Zion Cemetery, where a vault hidden in the hillside was a stop on the Underground Railroad.

Opposite: School teacher Emma Brown's former house

Above: First Baptist Church of Georgetown Below: Alfred and Hannah Pope house

Walk down 27th Street NW and left on O Street NW, where you'll come across ❷ ROSE PARK RECREATION CENTER & TENNIS COURTS, originally designated for Black residents. Official records show a donation from the Ancient Order of the Sons and Daughters of Moses in 1918 for the plot of land, with instructions for it to be used by the Black children who lived in the area. By 1930, Blacks and whites enjoyed Rose Park together. But DC was still a segregated city, and the Parks and Recreation Department tried to segregate the playground. But Black and white Georgetowners protested and prevailed. Years later, the city recorded Rose Park as the first integrated park in DC, but it was not due to the city's actions.

Rose Park is also notable as the home court for Margaret and Roumania Peters, two Black tennis stars of the late 1930s through the early 1950s who lived nearby. As young girls, they could often be seen playing at the park, where they earned the nicknames "Pete" and "Repeat."

"These young girls were the precursors to Althea Gibson, Venus and Serena Williams, and Naomi Osaka, in the sense that they would not allow the restrictions and barriers placed in their way to stop them from achieving their goals," sports historian Jarricka Ward told *The Washington Informer*. The sisters gained some fame and crowds gathered to see them play. While stationed in DC during World War II, actor Gene Kelly often played tennis with the sisters. In 2015, the DC Government dedicated the tennis courts to them.

Backtrack on O Street NW, right on 30th Street NW, and left on P Street NW. Continue to 3044 P Street NW, ❸ HOME OF EMMA V. BROWN, a native Washingtonian, who opened The School for Colored Girls in her home to teach emancipated Black children. "With education we can no longer be oppressed," she wrote in an 1858 letter to abolitionist William Lloyd Garrison. In 1864, Brown was hired as a teacher in the Little Ebenezer United Methodist Church, which still exists on Capitol Hill, making her the first Black teacher to be employed by DC Public Schools.

Turn left on 31th Street, then left again on O Street and continue until you reach 2900 O Street NW. This house on the corner belonged to ④ **ALFRED AND HANNAH POPE,** a formerly enslaved couple. After they were freed, the Popes remained in Georgetown, and Alfred took on the job of "town scavenger." He would go on to become a real estate magnate, politician, and philanthropist. He owned coal and lumber yards on 29th Street, as well as five single-family houses and five tenements in Georgetown. Alfred Pope became one of the most influential Black Georgetowners of the mid-to-late 19th century.

Continue down 29th Street NW. Established in 1814 by free and enslaved Black parishioners, the ⑤ **MOUNT ZION UNITED METHODIST CHURCH** is the oldest Black church in Georgetown and one of the oldest in DC. Mount Zion is thought to have been a station in the Underground Railroad, and the church records give some credence to this idea. The current location is on land purchased from Alfred Pope.

At the next corner, turn left on Dumbarton Street NW to the corner of 27th Street NW to find another important Black church. ⑥ **FIRST BAPTIST CHURCH OF GEORGETOWN** was founded in 1856 by Reverend Sandy Alexander (1818–1902), a former slave who came to Georgetown to start a Baptist church. When he arrived, he found only two Baptists but quickly met converts. With a donation of land, he built a small, frame structure called "The Ark." When trustees went to make the first payment on the note, the receipt was made out to the "First African Baptist Church." Trustee William T. Brown refused to accept it, insisting that he represented the "First Baptist Church," one church for all. The receipt was torn up, and a corrected one was written. The church continues to be an active congregation.

Turn right onto 27th Street NW. Walk, then turn right onto Olive Street NW. The yellow house at 2706 Olive Street NW is the former ⑦ **HOME OF FAMED CHEF AND COOKBOOK AUTHOR JULIA CHILD** (1912–2004). Child lived here from 1948 to 1959, teaching cooking classes and working on her legendary cookbook,

Opposite: Famed chef and cookbook author Julia Child's former house

Above: The former Phillips School was built to teach Black children in Herring Hill.

Mastering the Art of French Cooking. The 1869 house was built by Edgar Murphy, a Black carpenter from West Virginia, according to *The Washington Post.* In the 1870 Census, Murphy was listed as a 46-year-old carpenter, and the house was valued at $2,000—a high figure for the times. Murphy and his wife lived there with their seven children for more than 40 years. The house sold for $3.3 million in 2022.

Now, let's head to 2735 Olive Street NW. The former ❽ **PHILLIPS SCHOOL** was built in 1890 to educate Black children in Herring Hill. It was named after abolitionist Wendell Phillips (1811–1884). Despite its convenient location, many students did not want to attend due to fears of mosquitoes and malaria from Rock Creek. Declining property values and a lack of enrollment forced the school to close around 1950. It was turned into condominiums in 2002.

It is noteworthy and more than a bit ironic that Georgetown University, the area's most prestigious institution of higher learning, has a national landmark named to honor a Black man. Jesuit priest Patrick F. Healy (1834–1910) was born enslaved in 1873. He "passed" his way to become president of the university. Healy Hall is named in his honor. Today, the university openly acknowledges Healy as the first Black president of a predominantly white university.

Continue walking and turn left at 30th Street NW. ❾ **DR. JAMES FLEET,** a violinist and one of three Black physicians in Georgetown, purchased the house at 1208 30th Street in 1843 and ran a music school for African Americans. He studied medicine under the sponsorship of the American Colonization Society, which sought to send formerly enslaved people back to Africa, but Fleet refused to emigrate after his training. Instead, he stayed and began teaching. He opened his school in 1836.

Head to M Street NW and turn left. At the corner of 29th and M Streets NW is the former ❿ **ALFRED LEE FEED AND GRAIN STORE.** It was owned by Alfred Lee, one of Georgetown's more prosperous African Americans, who was also the half-brother of General Robert E. Lee, the Confederate general during the Civil War. Alfred Lee bought advertisements nearly every month in local papers for his business, which undoubtedly played a hand in his success. It was reported in an 1865 issue of the *Washington National Intelligencer* that Lee had purchased the British Legation building that the government had been leasing on H Street. When he died in 1868, Lee left an estate of $300,000, (the equivalent of $5.7 million today) mostly in real estate. The family operated the business into the 1940s. In 1942, *The Washington Star* noted that the business was the "oldest business among Negroes in America."

The Black population of Georgetown greatly declined in 1930 to less than nine percent by the 1960 Census, and the racial diversity that had been so much a part of Georgetown's historical character was virtually lost. Today, only a handful of native Black Georgetowners remain, and ⓫ **SANDLOT GEORGETOWN,** located near the Four Seasons hotel, is one of just a few Black-owned businesses. The shipping container bar and event space, part of a local empire, is owned by DC native Ian Callender who was named a "Washingtonian of the Year" in 2022. Black Georgetowners made significant contributions in shaping the neighborhood's identity. In the churches and other historic buildings where businesses and education thrived, reminders of their legacy abound.

1 HERRING HILL HISTORIC MARKER
2701 P Street NW
Washington, DC 20007

2 ROSE PARK RECREATION CENTER & TENNIS COURTS
2609 Dumbarton Street NW
Washington, DC 20007
www.dpr.dc.gov/page/rose-park-recreation-center

3 HOME OF EMMA V. BROWN
3044 P Street NW
Washington, DC 20007

4 ALFRED & HANNAH POPE'S FORMER HOME
2900 O Street NW
Washington, DC 20007

5 MOUNT ZION UNITED METHODIST CHURCH
1334 29th Street NW
Washington, DC 20007
www.mtzionumcdc.org

6 FIRST BAPTIST CHURCH OF GEORGETOWN
2624 Dumbarton Street NW
Washington, DC 20007
www.firstbaptistgtown.org

7 JULIA CHILD'S FORMER HOUSE
2706 Olive Street NW
Washington, DC 20007

8 PHILLIPS SCHOOL
2735 Olive Street NW
Washington, DC 20007

9 DR. JAMES FLEET'S FORMER HOUSE
1208 30th Street
Washington, DC 20007

10 ALFRED LEE FEED & GRAIN STORE
2900–2908 M Street NW
Washington, DC 20007

11 SANDLOT GEORGETOWN
2715 Pennsylvania Avenue NW
Washington, DC 20007
www.sandlotgeorgetown.com

Above: Historic marker and signage

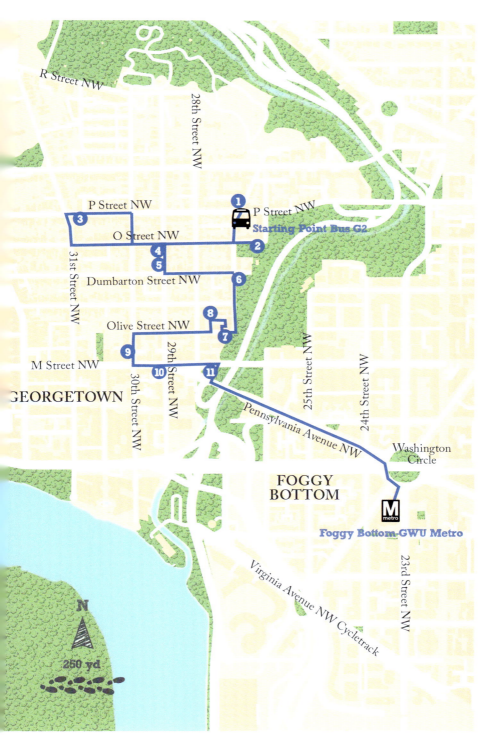

11 Grand Hotels Walk

History, ghosts, and radiant decor

> **BEST TIME:** Any season or time of day
> **DISTANCE:** Approximately 1 mile
> **ROUTE DESCRIPTION:** Flat and easy – take time to stop for tea or a cocktail
> **START:** Metro at Farragut North (Red Line)
> **END:** Metro at Metro Center (Blue, Orange, Red, Silver Lines)

Hotels of a certain age are repositories of local, and in DC's case, international history and lore. These grand dames certainly have stories to tell, though appearances may be deceiving. Sometimes their elegance camouflages scandal and secret events, and sometimes an uninteresting façade conceals a state-of-the-art interior.

Begin at the ❶ MAYFLOWER HOTEL, named after the original Mayflower and known as Washington's "second best address" behind only the White House, according to President Truman. When it opened, the press noted that it contained more gold leaf than any other building except the Library of Congress. Peek inside the Grand Ballroom, which, though small by today's standards, is one of the city's grandest. From Room 776 on the eve of his 1933 inauguration, Franklin D. Roosevelt declared, "The only thing we have to fear is fear itself." Look for historic images and artifacts in the display cases on the mezzanine.

Meetings of the Women's Organization for National Prohibition Reform and the 1931 Democratic National Committee held here proved to be pivotal in the repeal of Prohibition. Upon repeal, the hotel immediately paid the $1,000 fee for its liquor license. Pop in for a swig at Edgar's Bar, named for FBI Director J. Edgar Hoover, who loved the original and could be found there with his cronies regularly. When President Truman needed to find him, he would head straight for this bar.

Opposite: The Mayflower Hotel, DC's "second best address"

Above: Charles Sumner School Museum tells history through the lens of DC public schools.

Exit the hotel to your right on Connecticut Avenue and turn right on M Street, passing St. Matthew's Cathedral. At the corner of 17th Street NW is the ❷ CHARLES SUMNER SCHOOL MUSEUM and archive of the history of DC Public Schools. The award-winning building is named for the vehement abolitionist senator from Massachusetts who was notoriously severely caned by pro-slavery Representative Preston Brooks after giving a fiery speech in the chamber. Sumner (1811–1874) fought unsuccessfully to keep DC schools and public places from being segregated throughout his tenure in Congress.

At the end of the block on the left of 16th Street NW is ❸ THE JEFFERSON HOTEL. There are many nods to Thomas Jefferson (1743–1826) in the collection of documents that grace a lobby wall. Stroll through the Book Room to find an arrangement that resembles his library in Monticello. Authors who have stayed here have gifted signed copies of their books to these shelves to accompany titles that would have been of interest to Jefferson himself. It is one of 34 buildings designed by architect Jules Henri de Sibour (1872–1938), whose Beaux Arts inclinations brought elegant and ornate French architecture to DC's skyline in the early 1900s.

During World War II, the US Air Force flew reconnaissance missions over DC to identify potential targets that might attract German air attacks. During a recent renovation, the lobby skylight that had been covered over at that time to avoid detection from above was once again exposed.

Down two blocks and across 16th Street, passing the original National Geographic headquarters building, University Club, and the Russian Ambassador's house, you'll find the relatively nondescript ❹ CAPITAL HILTON HOTEL, originally Statler Hotel. It began as an idea during a conversation in 1940 between a hotel company board member and a construction magnate during the annual Gridiron Club dinner of captains of industry. There were few luxury hotels in wartime DC, while media, military, and diplomats poured into the city. So the partners agreed to build this hotel together. Statler opted to open the doors quietly to the media before the Department of the Navy could annex rooms. By the time the hotel was officially opened, all the rooms were sold out.

It can be noted in the Presidential ballroom that it was a work of au courant construction that includes an eight-foot-thick, bomb-proof north wall against which the dais is set for events when a US president is the guest of honor. There was once a hydraulic auto lift designed to get President Franklin Roosevelt's car from the ground to the ballroom level so that he could be settled discreetly in his wheelchair at the dais before the doors opened. And it was the largest air-conditioned hotel in the world. Statler Hotels sold it to Hilton Hotels in 1951 in the biggest commercial real estate sale in US history.

Just across K Street stands the ❺ ST. REGIS HOTEL, an elegant Beaux-Arts building by developer Harry Wardman who wanted to create a hotel to rival the best hotels in Europe. It has a stunning, gilded, Florentine interior. The concierge might allow you to peek inside the Astor Ballroom, with its embossed-leather ceilings. It's an ode to John Jacob Astor IV (1865–1912), who built the first St. Regis Hotel in New York City and went down with the *Titanic*. Cordell Hull (1871–1955), the longest serving Secretary of State, Nobel Peace Prize laureate, and architect of the United Nations, lived here for a stint during World War II. President Reagan's barber shop was on the lower level, and JFK came here regularly for his favorite dessert, the chocolate parfait. Perle Mesta, Equal Rights Amendment activist, political socialite, and ambassador, hosted her pink-themed galas in the ballroom for years. She was the inspiration for the term "Hostess with the Mostest" and Irving Berlin's musical *Call Me Madam*.

Step out to the left and walk along the two blocks of blazing yellow letters that comprise ❻ BLACK LIVES MATTER PLAZA, a permanent addition to the landscape after 2020 protests for racial equality and against police brutality.

At the end of the plaza, the stately ❼ HAY-ADAMS HOTEL stands on the site where the homes of best friends John Hay (1838–1905) and Henry Adams (1838–1918), a descendant of two presidents, once stood side by side. This was the first hotel in the city with air conditioning in its main ballroom, the Hay-Adams Room, and features one of the most elegant lobbies in town, with Tudor and Elizabethan motifs throughout. Views of the White House from guest room windows and the rooftop have been seen in movies, such as *In the Line of Fire* (1993) and *Wag the Dog* (1997).

Hay was President Lincoln's personal secretary, and he later served as ambassador to the United Kingdom and twice as Secretary of State. Adams was a Harvard history professor. The hotel's Hay-Adams Room, with some of the original woodwork, is a replica of the common room that conjoined the two original homes. This was where the two friends hosted salons for the literati in their "Five of Hearts Social Club," named for the two men, their wives Clara Hay and Marian Adams, and friend Clarence King, a geologist and the first director of the US Geological Survey. It is speculated that Hay and Adams were more than friends, which is perhaps why Adams' wife Clover poisoned herself with cyanide and is said to haunt the hotel from time to time.

Clockwise from top left: Hotel Washington; lobby of St Regis Hotel; Black Lives Matter Plaza; Willard Hotel lobby with state seals in the ceiling; Presidential plates at the Capital Hilton Hotel; The Jefferson Hotel

Continue walking diagonally to the left and across Lafayette Park, or President's Park, where influential residents included former First Lady Dolley Madison (1768–1849) in the yellow mansion on the northeast corner, and Admiral Stephen Decatur (1779–1820) on the northwest corner, the first private residence in the Presidents' neighborhood, now the home of the White House Historical Association.

Turn left onto Pennsylvania Avenue, right on 15th Street NW, and then left on F Street NW. On the modern building at the northeast corner of F Street is a plaque marking the location of the 1799 ❽ RHODES TAVERN that was thought to be the oldest commercial building in the city at the time of its demise in 1984. It had served as several different taverns, inns, townhall, bank, and press club until a developer demolished it despite a years-long battle to preserve it.

Cross the street and look up at the façade of the 1917 Beaux Arts ❾ HOTEL WASHINGTON, and pause to examine its impressive sgraffito ornamentation. The VUE Rooftop offers craft cocktails and breathtaking views of the White House and the Washington Monument. The hip, artsy lobby contrasts with the elegant exterior.

At the end of the block, it is impossible simply to walk past the majestic, Second Empire-style ❿ WILLARD HOTEL. So go inside at the F Street entrance at the top of magnificent Peacock Alley, where you'll find the tiny gallery that shares the hotel's remarkable history. President Lincoln endorsed his first presidential paycheck over to the hotel to pay his hefty pre-inaugural bill. Seek out your state seal on the ceiling of the lobby, where President Ulysses S. Grant (1822–1885) spent hours partaking of the cigars and brandy that his wife forbade in the White House. It was he who popularized the British term "lobbyist" when referring to the pesky hangers-on who constantly attempted to curry his favor. Martin Luther King, Jr. set up shop in the lobby here in 1963 for fear of surveillance in his hotel room. This is where he put the finishing touches on his "I Have a Dream" speech the night before he delivered it from the steps of the Lincoln Memorial.

Opposite: The Hay-Adams Hotel, named for best friends

In the Willard's Round Robin Bar, enjoy a perfect Mint Julep, thanks to Kentucky Senator Henry Clay (1777–1852). In a fit of annoyance over not being able to get a proper cocktail, he taught the hotel bartenders how to make one. Each Thanksgiving, two VITs (Very Important Turkeys) to be pardoned by the President are hosted in their own suites prior to the ceremony on the White House Lawn. And most years Millie the duck lays her eggs in the courtyard, which are diligently protected by the hotel's engineering team. Outside the front door, peruse the array of plaques on the building that mark the historic events that have taken place here.

❶ MAYFLOWER HOTEL
1127 Connecticut Avenue NW
Washington, DC 20036
www.themayflowerhotel.com

❷ CHARLES SUMNER SCHOOL MUSEUM
1201 17th Street NW
Washington, DC 20036
www.osse.dc.gov/page/charles-sumner-school-museum-and-archives

❸ THE JEFFERSON HOTEL
1200 16th Street NW
Washington, DC 20036
www.jeffersondc.com

❹ THE CAPITAL HILTON HOTEL
1001 16th Street NW
Washington, DC 20036
www.historichotels.org/us/hotels-resorts/capital-hilton/history

❺ ST. REGIS HOTEL
923 16th Street NW
Washington, DC 20006
www.historichotelsthenandnow.com/carltonwashington

❻ BLACK LIVES MATTER PLAZA
16th Street NW,
between K & H Streets NW
Washington, DC 20006
www.washington.org/visit-dc/black-lives-matter-plaza

❼ HAY-ADAMS HOTEL
800 16th Street NW
Washington, DC 20006
www.hayadams.com/our-hotel/history

❽ RHODES TAVERN HISTORIC MARKER
1495 F Street NW
Washington, DC 20004
historicsites.dcpreservation.org/items/show/506

❾ HOTEL WASHINGTON
515 15th Street NW
Washington, DC 20004
www.thehotelwashington.com/washington-dc-hotels/washington-dc-history

❿ WILLARD HOTEL
1401 Pennsylvania Avenue NW
Washington, DC 20004
www.washington.intercontinental.com/history

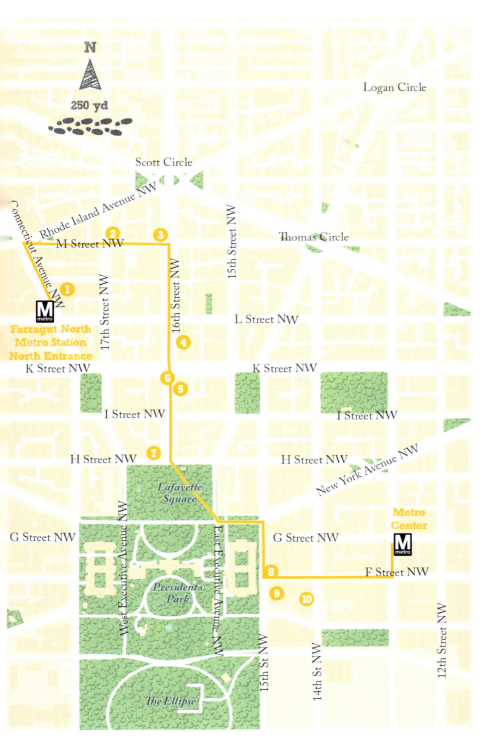

CAPITOL HILL SE

12 __ Hidden Alley Houses Walk
Secrets of these backstreet spaces revealed

> **BEST TIME:** Any season or time of day
> **DISTANCE:** 1.1 miles
> **ROUTE DESCRIPTION:** Flat but winding through alleys, so watch for cars
> **START:** Metro at Eastern Market (Blue, Orange, Silver Lines)
> **END:** Metro at Potomac Avenue (Blue, Orange, Silver Lines)

In most of DC, the alleyways tucked behind rows of houses serve only as trash collection points or access to parking spots. But a few have hidden surprises: small dwellings that people call home!

In early plans for Washington, narrow, 15-foot-wide passageways led from the edges of a block into wider, 30-foot passages in the interior, dubbed "blind alleys" because they weren't easily visible from the streets. As the city developed and row houses were built around the edges of blocks, the spaces on the inside were seen as wasted. Property owners subdivided their lots and put up livery stables, barns, warehouses, tin shops, and sheds in the alleys.

They built homes here, too, namely small, two-story houses, usually 10 to 12 feet wide and with entrances off alley streets too narrow to maneuver a modern car through. They have been a cornerstone of DC real estate since the 1780s as a way to provide affordable housing to working-class families.

Between 1865 and 1867, Charles Gessford and Stephen Flanagan, two property owners, partnered to build 16 attached row houses on 11th Street SE (132–144 11th Street SE). Gessford had the row houses built for his Philadelphia native wife to aid with her homesickness, which resulted in ❶ **PHILADELPHIA ROW**. The buildings had flat fronts of innovative machine-made pressed bricks. The bricks' smooth surfaces and crisp edges contrasted with the coarser

Opposite: Homes on "Philadelphia Row"

Above: Gessford Court sign Below: Mott's Market

texture of older ones and would replace them in most construction on Capitol Hill, and across the city. Flat roofs invisible from the streets, modest brackets at the cornice line, four-panel doors, and larger window panes further distinguished Philadelphia Row from its Hill forebears. This development predates by several decades much of the construction around Lincoln Park, which is located nearby.

Now, continue on and look for the Gessford's alley dwellings. Head south on 11th Street SE toward Independence Avenue SE. After you pass River Rock Court SE, Gessford Court SE will be next on your immediate left. Walk into the alley until you reach a cream-colored building and the "Gessford Court" sign hanging overhead.

❷ **GESSFORD COURT,** tucked in an alley on 11th Street between C Street and Independence Avenue SE, is easy to miss. But this tiny alley community has been around since the Civil War era. Charles Gessford (1831–1894) was one of the most well-known architects to design homes on Capitol Hill in the late 19th century. The Maryland native built more houses in Capitol Hill than any other builder, and most of his work was completed between 1875 and 1895.

He built 11 alley dwellings, numbers 1 through 21 Gessford Court. They are two-story homes on 12- by 24-foot lots, with a common brick exterior, each painted a different color. The homes' interiors have similar floor plans as well. The entrance usually leads into the kitchen, with a dining-living area downstairs and bedrooms upstairs. In the early days, the houses had no interior plumbing. Residents carried water into their houses from a water pump in the courtyard and used privies in the backyards. They relied on kerosene lamps for lighting and a stove for both cooking and heating. In the evenings, the residents, most likely a working-class Black or immigrant family, would have congregated around these light and heat sources.

Some of the alleys were given colorful names, like Hog Alley, Tin Can Alley, Louse Alley, Moonshine Alley, Pig Alley, Pork Steak Alley, and Cabbage Alley. Although originally without a name, this particular alley became known as Tiger Alley. Shortly after Gessford's death, in hopes of quieting the alley, its name was changed to

Gessford Street and eventually Gessford Court. But the name had little impact on the inhabitants, who continued to be known mainly for their rowdy behavior.

The most exciting time for Gessford Court was from the late '50s until the early '70s when ❸ **ADAM CLAYTON POWELL, JR.** (1908–1972), a US Representative and influential civil rights leader from Harlem, made his home here while Congress was in session. Powell renovated the homes, keeping number 16 to live in and 18 to rent out. Powell's son reminisced about black cars rolling into the alley carrying the likes of Barry Goldwater and Hubert Humphrey, who would crowd the pup-tent-size living room for political meetings shrouded in cigar smoke.

Why choose tiny Gessford for such big men? "Because reporters couldn't find this place," Powell said. Gessford wasn't on city maps for a long time, and even now, Google Maps misidentifies it as running east–west and not north–south.

Head out of the alley toward 12th Street SE. Erected in 1916 as a neighborhood store, the building on the corner to the right at 232 12th Street SE, now ❹ **MOTT'S MARKET,** has hosted stores ever since. It was built and owned by Jewish immigrants fleeing repression in Russia. The store was Jewish-owned, as were many of DC's corner stores at the time, for much of its history. The building's architect and contractor, Israel Diamond, built many of DC's Safeway stores.

The store became Mott's Market when the name first appeared on a liquor application in 1962 for a new proprietor, Murray Wollstein. Mott's was a modification from his Yiddish nickname "Mottel." When the store closed and went up for sale in March 2022, neighbors managed to gather donations and investors, and successfully purchased the space to keep Mott's Neighborhood Market open.

From here, continue right on 12th Street SE. Cross South Caroline Avenue SE, then turn left onto C Street SE. Adolf Cluss Court SE will be on your right. Along the way, notice the front yards, which

Opposite: Adam Clayton Powell, Jr.'s alley homes

give the neighborhood its cozy and communal feel. Curiously, front yards here and in many other parts of DC are actually public property. Pierre L'Enfant's vision for the capital city called for expansive boulevards and majestic streets, like the grand boulevards in Europe. But that high vision felt incongruous in the intimate and residential neighborhoods, where row homes were only two or three stories tall. In the 1870s, Congress passed the Parking Act and the Projection Act, which shrank local residential streets and created broad setbacks in front of homes, which are still public rights-of-way designated for private use. "Parking" in this case has nothing to do with vehicles—they would have been horse-drawn at that time. Nineteenth-century legislators envisioned residential streets lined with green, miniature "parks," not cars.

Compared to Gessford Court, where the original alley dwellings still remain, alleys like Adolf Cluss Court historically served as back entrances, storage, or horse passageways. Decades ago, alleys had a lot of life coursing through them, lined by blacksmiths, cobblers, bakeries, furniture upholstery places, and bicycle repair shops. Thanks to efforts by the Capitol Hill Restoration Society, alley lots and buildings like carriage houses and stables in the area are being converted into residential spaces are being preserved, keeping the alleys and buildings looking much the way they did in the early 19th century.

Today, Adolph Cluss Court has a mix of one-story garages and two-story carriage houses, many of which have been converted for residential use. It's named after DC architect Adolf Cluss (1825–1905), most well-known for designing the Smithsonian Castle and the nearby Eastern Market.

One of the modern-day residential projects revitalizing Capitol Hill's alleys is at the ❺ **NASH HOME,** the house with three beige-colored garage doors located ahead to your right. This 1920s warehouse belonged to the Steuart family, who owned an oil business and property throughout the city. It was originally used to store and distribute coal and ice to the neighborhood. When it was restored by Carl and Undine Nash in 2011–2012, the goal was to keep it looking as

Above: Front yards give the neighborhood a cozy, communal feel. Ironically, they are considered public property here and in other parts of DC.

much like the original industrial building as possible, according to the Urban Turf website. The building sits on the original footprint, and much of the brick and other materials were salvaged and reused.

The entry gate and front door, to your right as you make your way through the alley, are both repurposed pieces. The vast majority of alleys on Capitol Hill didn't have official directory names in the 19th century. The Nashes went through the ANC and DC Council to give their new home its own address.

Before exiting the alley onto D Street SE, take a look at the design of the iron window covering of the building to your right. It's actually a map. Can you tell what the map is showing you? The large square at the top is nearby Lincoln Park and the diagonal line near the bottom is Pennsylvania Avenue. The "H" shape near the lock is Cluss Court; the square by it represents the house you're currently visiting.

Now, turn right onto D Street SE and turn left when you reach 12 Street SE. Head toward Walker Court SE, which will be on your

127

right. Go into the alley and walk until you reach the split in the walkway. The alley dwelling is on the corner to your immediate left.

As you enter the alley, don't be surprised if you spot famous faces from local/national news and Hollywood movies milling about. Christopher Albert, a multiple Emmy, and White House News Photographer Association (WHNPA) award-winning Director of Photography, owns ❻ **STUDIOWERKSDC,** a photo and film production studio located in the fully restored, 1890s, detached carriage house ahead to the right.

The next stop is another residential alley conversion on the corner to your immediate left. Compared to the historic preservation dwelling at Cluss Court, ❼ **ALLEY CATCH,** the alley dwelling at 420 Walker Court behind 426 11th Street SE, is an award-winning example of a contemporary project in a historic alley. The original, three-bay, brick and wood structure was likely built in the early 1900s. Three other alley structures appearing on 1890 and 1908 historic maps were likely built in the 1880s, around the same time as many houses on this block.

The rundown building was turned into a modern dwelling with two separate apartments using materials that would look appropriate in an alley. Brick from a demolished wall was saved and reused to reconstruct a wall on the north side. Though much of the building is new, the historic brick parts of the façade preserve its connection to its past. The result of this effort is an intriguing blend of modern design and preserved and reused historic fabric.

Enjoying the different houses and gardens you pass, continue walking through the alley toward 11th Street SE, and turn left onto 11th Street SE. Next, turn left on Pennsylvania Avenue SE and then make a slight left onto E Street SE. From here, make your way to 502 13th/Peterbug Matthews Way SE.

❽ **PETER BUG SHOE AND LEATHER REPAIR ACADEMY,** which sits on land former First Lady Lady Bird Johnson do-

Opposite: Studiowerks DC sign

nated to the District, was founded over 40 years ago by John Matthews, who is known throughout DC as "Peter Bug," a nod to a Volkswagen Beetle he drove for years. The native son of the Southeast DC and master cobbler opened the shoe repair and academy to offer part-time employment to kids in the neighborhood and pass the art of shoe repair onto future generations. He has famously said his goal is to "Save souls and heel people," a play on words that connects his Shoe Repair Academy to activities that benefit those in need, especially children.

The Advisory Neighborhood Commission voted unanimously to designate Peter Bug Shoe Repair Academy as a DC Historical Landmark, and 13th Street SE was renamed in his honor in 2010.

After your visit here, continue walking along E Street SE. Turn left onto 15th Street SE, and then make a right onto ❾ **DUVALL COURT.** As you enter the alley, you can't help but notice the colorful mural that dominates the wall to the right. Look for the inspirational mural by Mimi Ton, who uses women's own words to tell the story of the fight for gender equality, from Sally Ride's "Weightlessness is a great equalizer," to Kamala Harris' "While I may be the first... I won't be the last."

Duvall Court SE is named for John H. Duvall who built seven brick, two-story dwellings in this alley in 1891. The buildings were home to Germans, who are thought to have worked in the nearby Capitol Brewery Company. According to Census records, the residents were all white in 1900. By 1910, the alley had one Black household, and by 1920, Black families lived in all the homes. Over time, people moved out of the alleys, and the buildings were torn down in 1968. When the zoning code changed in 2016, an investor gradually purchased all of the lots and requested permission to design a modern alley neighborhood. Duvall Court was born.

Just past the fence to the right, a cluster of seven modular-style row houses painted in white-grey-light turquoise now occupy this site. Designed by award-winning KUBE Architecture, these homes were built using one design prototype and customized as desired. The smallest of these houses is nine-feet wide, and some of the units have

Above: Alley home in Alley Catch Below: Peter Bug Shoe and Leather Repair Academy

a "flex space" on the main level that have Murphy beds and can be reconfigured with retractable walls. Most also have second-floor rear-facing balconies. Other amenities include walkable green roofs, parking on each lot, and lots of natural light. This type of prototype alley house is a model for future neighborhoods in DC and beyond.

Compare the design of alley dwellings you've seen on this walk: from the classic row house style on Gessford Court to the historic preservation styles in Adolf Cluss and Walter Courts, to the modern design of the building in Duvall Court. What similarities and differences do you recall? Which alley dwelling style do you prefer?

Today's alley dwellings are hardly affordable housing with homes on the market now going for well over $500,000. Alley dwellings that began in Washington about 120 years ago as housing for working-class whites, and which became slums for black residents for almost a century following the Civil War, have become, for the most part, an expensive and highly sought-after residence for affluent Washingtonians.

❶ PHILADELPHIA ROW
132–144 11th Street SE
Washington, DC 20003

❷ GESSFORD COURT
Off 11th Street between C Street & Independence Avenue SE
Washington, DC 20003

❸ ADAM CLAYTON POWELL, JR.'S FORMER HOMES
16 & 18 Gessford Court SE
Washington, DC 20003

❹ MOTT'S MARKET
232 12th Street SE
Washington, DC 20003

❺ NASH HOME
1237–1239 Rear C Street SE
Washington, DC 20003

❻ STUDIOWERKSDC
415B Walker Court SE
Washington, DC 20003
www.studiowerksdc.com

❼ ALLEY CATCH
420 Walker Court SE (behind 426 11th Street SE)
Washington, DC 20003

❽ PETER BUG SHOE AND LEATHER REPAIR ACADEMY
502 13th Street/
Peterbug Matthews Way SE
Washington, DC 20003
www.facebook.com/
PeterbugShoeLeatherAcademy

❾ DUVALL COURT
15 1/2 Street/Duvall Court SE
Washington, DC 20003

13 Latino at Heart Walk

Latin American culture thriving since the 1950s

> **BEST TIME:** Any season or time of day
> **DISTANCE:** 0.7 miles
> **ROUTE DESCRIPTION:** Flat and great for a moving feast
> **START:** Metro at Columbia Heights (Green Line)
> **END:** Metro at Columbia Heights (Green Line)

At the turn of the 20th century, the Pleasant Plains and Mount Pleasant Estates were distributed among the heirs, who sold off their tracts. Mount Pleasant emerged from the redistribution of land and has been an ever-changing, multi-ethnic neighborhood ever since. The first developers ignored the city's grid plan, utilizing existing farm roads and creating new ones that followed the hilly landscape. As a result, an 1893 law required future subdivisions to conform to L'Enfant's city plan. But the streets of Mount Pleasant still follow their own paths.

The neighborhood has attracted immigrants from Latin America and the Caribbean since the 1950s. Gentrification has been largely kept at bay here, and neighbors support each other's businesses and fight against national brand encroachment. Locals have created and sustained their own establishments here for decades, including some of the oldest family-run businesses in DC.

Affectionately called "La Manplesa," the Spanish pronunciation of Mount Pleasant, the community has spread into neighboring Columbia Heights and Adams Morgan neighborhoods. Your walk begins at Mount Pleasant and Harvard Streets NW.

Before you begin, though, take note of the stunning buildings that grace the surrounding corners, including ❶ **THE EMBASSY,** from whose balconies tenants can hear the sounds of the big cats and great apes at the National Zoo down the hill.

Opposite: GALA Hispanic Theatre

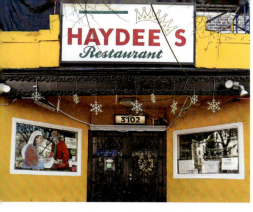

Clockwise from top left: Haydee's Restaurant; Streetcar Comes to Mount Pleasant callbox; Sacred Heart School art; El West shop; Corado's Restaurant; Embassy apartment building

On the next corner at Hobart Street NW is a late-19th-century fire call box adorned with a sculpture entitled ❷ *THE STREETCAR COMES TO MOUNT PLEASANT* that is part of the "Art on Call" project and offers a peek at life as this first suburb began to grow. Turn left to 1614 Hobart Street NW, which was the ❸ HOME OF "EL VIEJO" CARLOS ROSARIO, the formidable grassroots politician, who battled City Council to create and grow Latino community services into the strong organizations that remain today. His funeral in Adams Morgan in 1987 was one of the largest ever seen in DC. Renowned Salvadoran poet, activist, and educator Quique Aviles lived in an unknown group house on this street as a teenager in the 1980s and has since graced the greater community with his poetry, murals and education advocacy.

Return to the corner and turn left. As most of the businesses here are restaurants and retail stores, it is fitting to step in ❹ BOLD FORK BOOKS to peruse cookbooks of Latin American culinary delights to whet your appetite and inspire you in your own kitchen. Next door, ❺ ERCILIA'S RESTAURANT, a tiny corner spot, specializes in Salvadoran pupusas and serves as a gathering place for neighbors and late-night snackers.

Across Irving Street, go inside ❻ IRVING WINE & SPIRITS and pick up a bottle of Mount Pleasant Club Whiskey and its sister spirits, recently rebirthed from the early 1900s, when William D. Barry, a staunch anti-Prohibition advocate, owned the brand and sold it from his store a few blocks away. Local neophyte distillers were inspired to create Reboot Distillers after one of them found an old Club Whiskey bottle left behind by a 1911 construction crew in the home that he purchased on nearby 19th Street. Look across the street to the tiny, eclectic ❼ SUNS CINEMA, a great spot to check out uncommon flicks and an occasional Latino or Hispanic documentary or film at a matinee or evening show.

On the next block, the mainstay ❽ HAYDEE'S has been serving Salvadoran and Mexican dishes since 1990. Salvadoran owners Haydee Vanegas and chef Mario Alas gleefully work alongside their staff in this social establishment filled with live music, where you can enjoy a meal or a beer and a spin around the dance floor to everything from mariachi to jazz and rock.

For over 40 years, the corner of Kenyon and Mount Pleasant Streets has been the spot for ❾ LOS ESQUINEROS, or "the corner guys." Mostly Salvadorans and Mexicans, these men congregate here to play checkers and dominos, and discuss politics and home. They're happy to chat with new arrivals in the community, offering insights on how to navigate many aspects of life here. Mostly, though, they simply enjoy hanging out among friends. Many have been interviewed over the years by the Smithsonian Folklife Festival and the DC History Center, both of which have preserved their oral histories. They are circumspect with people they don't know, but you are welcome to strike up a conversation and share a story or two. In the building directly across the street lived ❿ MAMÁ TEY, a Salvadoran woman who was a mother to all who came from Central America, according to neighborhood legend. Her door was always open, and comfort food was always on the stove.

Adjacent is ⓫ LA CLÍNICA DEL PUEBLO, in a lively colored building, begun here as an all-volunteer clinic created by Salvadoran and American health advocates to provide bilingual health services for displaced Central Americans whose access to care was restricted by economic, language, and cultural barriers.

Across the street is a historic marker that commemorates ⓬ CASA DILONÉ, now Revo Nails, the first grocery store opened in the neighborhood. Though the bodega closed in 1998, it was once a mainstay of the local business community. Casa Diloné was owned by Puerto Rican Francisca Marrero Diloné and her Dominican husband Félix, who lived above the store with their six children, all of whom worked in the bodega. They offered items imbued with the flavors of home for Latino and Caribbean immigrants and embassy staffers alike. The store was a magnet for Spanish speakers and those seeking Francisca's legendary holiday treats. It also was the catalyst for other Latino-owned businesses to open on Mount Pleasant Street.

Above: La Clínica del Pueblo–La Casa Health Action Center
Belwo left: Mamá Tey always had comfort food on the stove here
Belwo right: Ercilia's Restaurant and pupuseria

Walk up Mount Pleasant Street and pop into ⑬ **EL WEST**. Owner Veronica is an ebullient Salvadoran, whose shop has morphed from a vendor of Mexican cowboy boots and full Western wear to a jam-packed shop for boho clothing, jeans, and accessories. But don't worry – she still sells beautiful Mexican boots and other cool kicks. Her team is beloved for their great service and generous philanthropy.

At the corner go right on Lamont Street, where the ⑭ **MOUNT PLEASANT LIBRARY** down the block offers bilingual and Spanish events and readings. Go inside to see the beautifully muraled children's reading area and its joyful array of bilingual books, including some written by local youth authors. Double back to the corner, where ⑮ **LEON'S SHOE REPAIR** is now owned by the son of the Guatemalan cobbler who opened it, and whose long-time customers still insist it is the best cobbler shop in town.

José Corado arrived from Guatemala and opened his tiny restaurant ⑯ **CORADO'S** over 40 years ago. He is the cook serving up typical comfort food like sopa de res and fluffy tamales. Server Marisol explains that the food is similar to Mexican fare, except that it's not "picante." Corado's is one of many long-standing spots frequented by locals, who are the keepers of many neighborhood stories.

Just outside, look up to see the fading ⑰ **HELLER'S BAKERY** sign painted on the building that once housed the city's oldest bakery, known for its notoriously mouthwatering apple and blueberry turnovers, fresh every day. A little further on, turn right into the alley, where the frequently rotating ⑱ **LOST ORIGINS OUTSIDE GALLERY** is a regularly changing and unexpected showplace for photography, painting, street art and graphics.

Continue on and turn right on Park Road to mid-block. In its early years, GALA Hispanic Theatre (Grupo de Artistas Latino Americanos) was given the auditorium at ⑲ **SACRED HEART SCHOOL** to fix up and call home. They stayed here for years until the school needed the space again.

Opposite: Leon's Shoe Repair

Above: Lost Origins Outside Gallery Below: Mount Pleasant Library

GALA, a pillar of Latino performing arts, is now housed in the historic ⑳ TIVOLI THEATRE three blocks east, and their performances are not to be missed. American Rebecca and Argentine Hugo Medrano started GALA in 1976 in response to the influx of artists fleeing repressive regimes in Latin America, and they have turned this diminutive space into one of the finest showcases for known, world-premier, and children's bilingual and Spanish-language plays written by renowned playwrights and newcomers. Buy a ticket and a glass of wine and enjoy a show that is new to you. Performances are surtitled in English or Spanish depending on the language being spoken onstage. Rebecca gleefully says, "Language is key to cultural heritage."

❶ THE EMBASSY
1613 Harvard Street NW
Washington, DC 20009

❷ *THE STREETCAR COMES TO MOUNT PLEASANT CALL BOX*
NW corner of Mount Pleasant Street NW & Hobart Street NW
Washington, DC 20009

❸ CARLOS ROSARIO'S HOME
1314 Hobart Street NW
Washington, DC 20009

❹ BOLD FORK BOOKS
3064 Mount Pleasant Street NW
Washington, DC 20009
www.boldforkbooks.com

❺ ERCILIA'S RESTAURANT
3070 Mount Pleasant Street NW
Washington, DC 20009
erciliasrestaurantwashington.cafecityguide.website

❻ IRVING WINE & SPIRITS
3100 Mount Pleasant Street NW
Washington, DC 20010
www.reboot-bev.com/history

❼ SUNS CINEMA
3107 Mount Pleasant Street NW
Washington, DC 20010
www.sunscinema.com

❽ HAYDEE'S RESTAURANT
3102 Mount Pleasant Street NW
Washington, DC 20010
www.haydees.com

❾ LOS ESQUINEROS
NW corner of Mount Pleasant & Kenyon Streets NW
Washington, DC 20010

❿ MAMÁ TEY
3149 Mount Pleasant Street NW
Washington, DC 20010

⓫ LA CLÍNICA DEL PUEBLO – LA CASA HEALTH ACTION CENTER
3166 Mount Pleasant Street NW
Washington, DC 20010
www.lcdp.org

⓬ CASA DILONÉ
(now Revo Nails)
3161 Mount Pleasant Street NW
Washington, DC 20010

⓭ EL WEST
3167 Mount Pleasant Street NW
Washington, DC 20010

⓮ MOUNT PLEASANT LIBRARY
3160 16th Street NW
Washington, DC 20010
www.dclibrary.org/plan-visit/mt-pleasant-library

⓯ LEON'S SHOE REPAIR
3201 Mount Pleasant Street NW
Washington, DC 20010

⓰ CORADO'S
3217 Mount Pleasant Street NW
Washington, DC 20010
www.coradosrestaurant.com

⓱ HELLER'S BAKERY SIGN
3221 Mount Pleasant Street NW
Washington, DC 20010

⓲ LOST ORIGINS OUTSIDE GALLERY
Alley adjacent to 3221 Mount Pleasant Street NW
Washington, DC 20010

⓳ SACRED HEART SCHOOL
1625 Park Road NW
Washington, DC 20010
www.sacredheartschooldc.com/history-and-mission

⓴ GALA HISPANIC THEATRE/TIVOLI THEATRE
3333 14th Street NW
Washington, DC 20010
www.galatheatre.org

Right: Bold Fork Books for Latin American cookbooks

14 — Lincoln's Ghost Walk
Imagine the president enjoying his old 'hood today

> **BEST TIME:** Daytime
> **DISTANCE:** Approximately 2.4 miles
> **ROUTE DESCRIPTION:** Gentle uphill and downhill grade, stop to shop and dance
> **START:** Metro at Georgia Avenue-Petworth (Green Line)
> **END:** Metro at Georgia Avenue-Petworth (Green Line)

President Abraham Lincoln spent the hot summers residing in a cottage on the grounds of the current Armed Forces Retirement Home during his tenure in Washington, DC from 1861 until 1865. He rode the three miles to the White House on horseback each day, down what is now Georgia Avenue NW and across today's Metro Center, pondering his deepest thoughts and often trying to evade his protective detail.

On those journeys, the president passed contraband camps of enslaved people escaping to reach the Union Army and sometimes stopped to say hello. He also passed hospitals and other reminders of the raging Civil War. On one occasion, he was shot at (for the first time), and the bullet pierced his stovepipe hat. He swore his security detail to keep this secret from his wife Mary. Poet Walt Whitman, who lived in DC for many years, documented exchanging salutations with the president periodically and later penned the poem "O Captain, My Captain" in his memory.

Now named Petworth after the estate that long ago occupied the area, it is a patchwork of architecture, churches, locally owned businesses, food stops, and bars owned mostly by Black and immigrant entrepreneurs. President Lincoln would certainly enjoy walking around this neighborhood today to see what it looks like in the 21st century. Conjure up his spirit to accompany you on your walk.

Opposite: President Lincoln and Old Abe at Lincoln's Cottage

Enter and start your walk with Abe at the eagle-adorned gates of ❶ **PRESIDENT LINCOLN'S COTTAGE,** built in 1842 by banker George W. Riggs (1813–1881) and loaned to the Lincolns. The Lincolns enjoyed the fresh air here, although the family was evacuated when nearby Fort Stevens came under Confederate fire in 1864. You can take a tour of the home, "a place for brave ideas," as they refer to it, and hear stories of Lincoln's life and major undertakings that transpired in this house, not the least of which was the writing of the Emancipation Proclamation. Educational programs, where respectful dialogue is encouraged, are offered throughout the year.

Leaving the cottage, just across Rock Creek Church Road NW is the ❷ **HITCHING POST,** a soul food spot favored for its delectable fried chicken and NPR host Kojo Nnamdi's namesake rum punch. It has been the epitome of a neighborhood hangout since it opened in 1967. Continue walking left down Rock Creek Church Road, the same route Lincoln would have ridden along. Peek in the gates to see the visually intriguing (but private) buildings of the old Soldiers' Home and imagine your conversation with the president as you go. On the grounds just before the intersection of Quincy Street is the ❸ **HEADWATER OF TIBER CREEK.** Though virtually non-existent here, it is still known to run under Constitution Avenue NW downtown.

When you reach the intersection of Georgia Avenue, turn left and walk three blocks to ❹ **EATS PLACE,** where you might encounter a fresh pop-up in this commercial kitchen and food incubator. On the corner, beloved owner Bill White has survived many setbacks to prevail in his stalwart ❺ **FISH IN THE NEIGHBORHOOD,** a good stop for a fried catfish sandwich or fried shrimp.

Continue down to vegan ❻ **CANE & COCONUT.** Guyanese owner Furtari serves enormous, refreshing containers of freshly juiced sugar cane and water from coconuts husked on the spot, great for taking on your walk. Imagine Presidents Lincoln and Obama chatting and drinking coconut water together here.

Opposite: Former 10th Precinct police station from which Houdini once escaped

Down two blocks and just across Georgia Avenue is where Mr. Lincoln today might be seen shaking his maracas with the neighbors in a salsa or bachata class, or at a monthly dance party in ❼ **SALSA WITH SILVIA DANCE STUDIO.** Silvia began teaching in her basement and has grown this into the largest Latin dance studio in the region.

Heading back uptown, two blocks north, ❽ **HOOK HALL** is a cool venue and bar where you might find lively world-music dance parties, winter-themed igloos, or pop-up markets. Stop in for a beer in the adjacent bar or book your igloo.

Up the block, turn left on Park Road to the ❾ **FORMER 10TH PRECINCT POLICE STATION.** On January 1, 1906, Police Chief Major Richard Sylvester invited escape artist Harry Houdini to visit this precinct and attempt a breakout following a performance downtown. Houdini had publicly remarked that he wished to show off his prison-escape skills, and the brand-new jail featured the most modern security and intricate combination locks of the day. After Houdini's required pre-check of the facility, the chief changed the cell locks at the last second. Totally nude, handcuffed in top-of-the-line Secret Service cuffs, behind five locks, and under unexpected circumstances, Houdini emerged from cell #3 in 18 minutes – fully clothed. He had had to break into the adjacent cell to retrieve his clothes and later commented that the cuffs were easy.

Double back, and turn left on Georgia Avenue to ❿ **MOM-N-POP ANTIQUES,** a fun destination for poking around for furniture, décor, and vintage barware for urban living.

On the left and two blocks up, the historic façade of ⓫ **OLD ENGINE COMPANY 24** embellishes the chiller plant for the Metro station below. In 1912, it was the first firehouse in DC to get all motorized fire engines, including pumper "Big Liz," which was the beginning of the end for horse-drawn pumpers in the District.

Continue three blocks north to another beloved Latino arts institution, ⓬ **CASA DE LA LUNA,** home of Teatro de la Luna, where adults and children can attend energetic, bilingual acting and

Clockwise from top left: Cane & Coconut; Timber Pizza; Salsa with Silvia Dance Studio; Hook Hall; head of Tiber Creek; Mom-N-Pop Antiques

Above: *(Here I Stand) In the Spirit of Paul Robeson* Below: Cookie Wear

poetry workshops, theatrical readings, and performances. As a resident of DC you can take some of the classes for free. Their larger theater productions are presented in Arlington, Virginia.

Saunter up two more blocks, and step inside the ❶❸ **PETWORTH NEIGHBORHOOD LIBRARY** where a composite stone and brass map of Petworth greets you in the main hall. It was an afterthought in the last renovation and one that garners lots of attention from visitors. President Lincoln would surely delight in seeing the modern, paved streetscape of his old stomping grounds mapped out where dirt roads prevailed in his time.

Diagonally across the avenue stands ❶❹ *(HERE I STAND) IN THE SPIRIT OF PAUL ROBESON,* a tribute to the renowned, outspoken polyglot actor, singer and activist who advocated for desegregation and workers' rights around the world, and the right of artists to express themselves freely. He was never a Washingtonian, but local artist Allen Uzikee Nelson felt that he earned this memorial in this predominantly Black city. Lincoln would have been a fan of the artist and agreed with him as well.

Cross Kansas Avenue NW and turn left on Upshur Street NW. Mid-block, vivid art in the window beckons you to enter ❶❺ **COOKIE WEAR,** owned by Michelle "Noodles" and Candace Smith, a mother and daughter team. They have filled the space with funky décor, much of it made by Michelle. You'll also find blazingly colorful streetwear and the coolest custom skateboards made by Candace. She can imagine President Lincoln in his stovepipe hat skating down Upshur Street. Stay tuned for an interesting new design.

Across the street, end your walk with a snack at neighborhood favorite ❶❻ **TIMBER PIZZA COMPANY.** Knowing that you and the ghost of President Lincoln have had a joyful jaunt through this dynamic part of the capital city, imagine that you and he would also enjoy attending all of the fun street markets and festivals that Petworth hosts throughout the year. As you walk back to the Metro along Upshur Street NW stop and take a photo in the alley in front of the brilliantly colorful *Petworth* mural. If you are lucky, Lincoln's ghost will photo bomb you.

PETWORTH NW

❶ PRESIDENT LINCOLN'S COTTAGE
140 Rock Creek Church Road NW
Washington, DC 20011
www.lincolncottage.org

❷ HITCHING POST
200 Upshur Street NW
Washington, DC 20011
www.thehpostrestaurant.com

❸ HEADWATER OF TIBER CREEK
Rock Creek Church Road
& Quincy Street NW
Washington, DC 20011

❹ EATS PLACE
3607 Georgia Avenue NW
Washington, DC 20010
eatsplace.com

❺ FISH IN THE NEIGHBORHOOD
3601 Georgia Avenue NW
Washington, DC 20010

❻ CANE & COCONUT
3501 Georgia Avenue NW
Washington, DC 20010
www.caneandcoconut.com

❼ SALSA WITH SILVIA DANCE STUDIO
3232 Georgia Avenue NW
Washington, DC 20010
www.salsawithsilvia.com

❽ HOOK HALL
3400 Georgia Avenue NW
Washington, DC 20010
www.hookhall.com

❾ FORMER 10TH PRECINCT POLICE STATION
750 Park Road NW
Washington, DC 20010

❿ MOM-N-POP ANTIQUES
3534 Georgia Avenue NW
Washington, DC 20010
www.attic.city/store/
mom-n-pop-antiques

⓫ OLD ENGINE COMPANY 24
3670 New Hampshire Avenue NW
Washington, DC 20010

⓬ CASA DE LA LUNA
4020 Georgia Avenue NW
Washington, DC 20011
www.teatrodelaluna.org

⓭ PETWORTH NEIGHBORHOOD LIBRARY
4200 Kansas Avenue NW
Washington, DC 20011
www.dclibrary.org/plan-visit/
petworth-library

⓮ *(HERE I STAND) IN THE SPIRIT OF PAUL ROBESON*
Georgia & Kansas Avenues NW
Washington, DC 20011

⓯ COOKIE WEAR
810 Upshur Street NW
Washington, DC 20011
www.cookiewearshop.com

⓰ TIMBER PIZZA COMPANY
809 Upshur Street NW
Washington, DC 20011
www.timberpizza.com

15 Locomotion History Walk

We sure have gotten around

BEST TIME: Sunny days when a splash of water feels good
DISTANCE: 1.4 miles
ROUTE DESCRIPTION: Flat with stops where kids can play
START: Metro at Eastern Market (Blue, Orange, Silver Lines) or Navy Yard (Green Line)
END: Metro at Eastern Market (Blue, Orange, Silver Lines) or Navy Yard (Green Line)

Like many neighborhoods, Navy Yard expanded thanks to the extension of the trolley lines. But it has been here since the city's beginning. The Navy Yard itself is the oldest shore base of the US Navy. It was established in 1799 as a shipbuilding facility for the Navy and has been in service ever since. During the Civil War, it was part of the fortification of the city against invaders like the British and was converted into the military's primary foundry of ordnance. It now houses Naval Operations and several other commands.

Your walk starts at the Greek Revival-style ❶ LATROBE GATE, named for Benjamin H. Latrobe (1764–1820), the celebrated architect who designed it and several other structures on base. This ceremonial entrance to the Navy Yard is only used by resident flag officers. It has been expanded a few times to accommodate the growing needs of the Marines and was later painted white to cover the array of brick colors.

Across M Street is the ❷ CAPITAL TURNAROUND, a unique event venue inside the Navy Yard Car Barn, which was the last stop on the Red Line of the Capital Transit Company. This is where streetcars turned around and came for repairs.

From the gate, walk right on M Street along the brick wall of the base, pausing to read the historic notes on banners, and passing the

Opposite: Navy Yard 6th Street Gate

Clockwise from top left: Yards Park Bridge; interactive elements of the Transportation Walk; Navy Yard; Capital Turnaround

❸ 6TH STREET GATE for a nicely framed view towards the Anacostia River. At the intersection with 4th Street SE, step into the remains of the **❹ SENTRY TOWER** to see contemporary portraits made of twisted wire, depicting the people who worked in the 21 shops that manufactured components for ordnance here.

Turn left on M Street SE and left on 3rd Street SE to Tingey Street SE, named for Thomas Tingey (1750–1829), the construction manager and longest serving Commandant of the Navy Yard, from 1804–1829, to explore the **❺ TRANSPORTATION WALK** that encircles the Department of Transportation. It's a visual and interactive four-segment timeline of US history through the lens of progress in North American transport. "Encounter and Exploration" begins in the 1600s with Native canoes and Captain John Smith, who was the first explorer to show the Anacostia on his 1607 map.

Walk east and turn left on 4th Street SE and left on M Street SE to "Industry and Expansion," which begins with 1812. The next block is "Greater Mobility" from 1900.

Just across at 2nd Street SE, enjoy a winter twirl around the meandering **❻ ICE RINK AT CANAL PARK.** In warm weather it is a serene lunch spot.

Go left on New Jersey Avenue SE and left on Tingey Street SE to the "Modern Era," from 1947, and the end of Transportation Walk.

The ships that adorn the top of the **❼ NAVAL FOUNTAIN** on Tingey Plaza look as though they are sailing across, and the different types of bridge cutouts that arch over intersections on Tingey Street depict the crossing of various modes of transportation. There are many opportunities along the way to sit on, turn, steer, and pump machinery for play and silly photos. That is their purpose. Markers, riddles, and trivia signs dot the way. For example, "What is green and located under your feet?" (Hint: It's not grass.)

Back on 3rd Street SE, turn right. The warm-weather **❽ YARDS PARK SPLASH POOL** earned some notoriety when the Capitals won the Stanley Cup in 2018, and the players took the Cup for a beer-filled swim. Stop to play behind the waterfall, which is on the site of the original ordnance foundry and is now the gateway to the Anacostia Riverfront Trail. The pool is an allusion to the canal that once ran from the river to the US Capitol as part of the L'Enfant city plan, and is designed to connect with the river.

Look to the right at the Beaux Arts-style building that houses DC Water's 1907 main ❾ **O STREET PUMPING STATION,** which has been upgraded to serve as a transport system of wastewater, an essential component of the Clean Rivers Project.

Continue left across the white Yards Park Bridge and saunter along the boardwalk by way of the ❿ **OVERLOOK** that evokes the sails of Tall Ships, to take in the views of the Anacostia. Take note of the undulating, wave-like benches made of wood and stone throughout the parks.

The ⓫ **ANACOSTIA RIVER,** once called the Eastern Branch of the Potomac River, was intended to be a deepwater port in the original plan for the city and its waterways. But because of its constant accumulation of silt, the long distance from the open ocean, and the increasing size of ships, it has only ever served small watercraft. Keep your eyes open for fire boats and fireworks barges on Nationals game days, festivals, and holidays.

As you walk, look across the Anacostia River and imagine that in the 1500s–1600s the Nacotchtank, or Anacostan, tribe lived in flourishing villages, where fishermen and fur traders paddled their canoes in these waters. Their name came from the Piscataway 'anaquashatanik', meaning "a town of traders." The word morphed into Anacostian, the namesake of the river itself. They encountered Captain John Smith (1580–1631) in the early 1600s and appeared on his 1624 map of the region. Subsequent settlers took land for tobacco plantations and pushed the Anacostian people to Analostan Island, now Theodore Roosevelt Island, and west. European-borne diseases took a heavy toll, and those few who survived were adopted into the Piscataway and Pamunkey tribes. They have no known descendants.

Once you reach the river side of the ⓬ **NAVY YARD BASE,** the view through the gates offers some of the innovations manufactured, used, and retired here, like the conning tower of the ⓭ *USS BALAO*

Above: Navy Yard waterfront along the Anacostia River *Below*: USS Balao

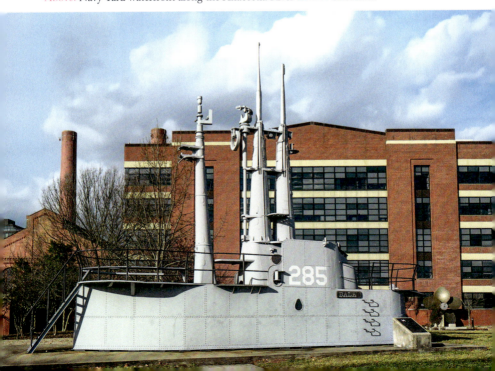

attack submarine that was once painted hot pink for its role in a popular comedy *Operation Petticoat* (1959) starring Cary Grant, Tony Curtis, and Gail O'Brien. The vessel was repainted navy gray for its retirement here.

During the War of 1812, the yard was a key supply link to fortify the capital city, but when Commodore Tingey saw the US Capitol on fire, at the hands of the invading British Army, he ordered the yard burned to the ground rather than have it captured. Only his quarters (Quarters A) and the Latrobe Gate survived. After the war, the yard shifted from shipbuilding to ordnance manufacturing and invention, at which it excelled for nearly a century.

Among the innovations built and installed in the Navy Yard were the country's first marine railway for the repair of large vessels, an alternative to a dry dock; one of the earliest steam engines to manufacture anchors, chain, and steam engines for warships; a model testing basin used by shipbuilders to test the effect of water on new hull designs; a wind tunnel; and the first successful shipboard catapult tested in the Anacostia.

Interestingly, in the early 1900s, the giant gears for the Panama Canal locks were cast here, and technicians experimented with designs for medical applications like prosthetic hands and molds for artificial eyes and teeth.

Across the parking lot, you can see the entrance of the ⓮ **NATIONAL MUSEUM OF THE US NAVY,** which houses such treasures as early metal diving suits, submersible and diving equipment prototypes, and scale ship models. It's also the home of the impressive Bathyscaphe Trieste, the submersible that has dived deeper than any other such vessel. To visit the museum and walk the base grounds, turn left, then left again on 11th Street to the O Street Gate and the Visitors' Center, where you must present ID and go through the process of admittance.

Or continue strolling through the neighborhood and enjoy a rooftop drink to take in the beautiful view from above.

Opposite: Canal Park, a splash park in summer and ice rink in winter

Above: Latrobe Gate
at the Navy Yard

❶ LATROBE GATE
Navy Yard
M & 8th Streets SE
Washington, DC 20003
www.history.navy.mil/content/history/
museums/nmusn/explore/photography/
washington-navy-yard/latrobe-gate.html

❷ CAPITAL TURNAROUND
700 M Street SE
Washington, DC 20003
www.capitalturnaround.com

❸ 6TH STREET GATE
M & 6th Streets SE
Washington, DC 20003

❹ SENTRY TOWER
M & 4th Streets SE
Washington, DC 20003

❺ TRANSPORTATION WALK
Department of Transportation
Tingey & 3rd Streets SE & 6 blocks
around the DOT buildings
Washington, DC 20003

❻ ICE RINK AT CANAL PARK
(in season)
200 M Street SE
Washington, DC 20003
www.skatecanalpark.com

❼ NAVAL FOUNTAIN
Tingey Plaza
New Jersey Avenue & Tingey Square SE
Washington, DC 20003

❽ YARDS PARK SPLASH POOL
3rd & Water Streets SE
Washington, DC 20003
www.capitolriverfront.org/yards-park

❾ O STREET PUMPING STATION
125 O Street SE
Washington, DC 20003
www.dcwater.com/projects/hqo

❿ THE OVERLOOK
Anacostia Riverwalk Trail
at White Bridge
Washington, DC 20003

⓫ ANACOSTIA RIVER
Washington, DC 20003

⓬ NAVY YARD BASE
Anacostia Riverwalk Trail
at 4th Street SE
Washington, DC 20003
www.history.navy.mil/
browse-by-topic/organization-and-
administration/installations/
washington-navy-yard.html

⓭ USS BALAO
Dahlgren Park in Navy Yard
Anacostia Riverwalk Trail
at Isaac Hull Avenue SE
Washington, DC 20376
www.history.navy.mil/content/
history/museums/nmusn/explore/
photography/ships-us/ships-usn-b/
uss-balao-ss-285.html

⓮ NATIONAL MUSEUM OF THE US NAVY
Navy Yard
736 Sicard Street SE
Washington, DC 20374
www.history.navy.mil/content/history/
museums/nmusn.html

CONGRESSIONAL CEMETERY SE

16 Native Americans Walk
Leaders came to DC on business; some never left

BEST TIME: Any season, daytime only
DISTANCE: Approximately 1.1 miles
ROUTE DESCRIPTION: Mostly flat, a bit rugged, some searching required
START: Metro at Potomac Avenue (Blue, Orange, Silver Lines)
END: Metro at Potomac Avenue (Blue, Orange, Silver Lines)

Washington, DC is built on land where the Nacotchtank People first lived. Once the capital was established, Native Americans faced peril not only during difficult cross-country travel, but also simply by coming into the city on behalf of their tribes to negotiate treaties, claim remuneration for unpaid government debts, and fight for tribal rights.

Congressional Cemetery has a history of accepting the remains of those who were not welcome elsewhere due to racism or the way they died. Today, there are 37 graves of tribal leaders here. Disease took most of them, their families, and delegates, but two died under very suspicious circumstances that remain unresolved over 150 years later. This walk is a bit of a scavenger hunt for graves, which are not always clearly marked. It is easiest to use the four cardinal directions here. The gatehouse is north. From the main gate, walk past the restrooms and turn east on the narrow path, then three rows east, and about 20 feet north. ❶ **WILLIAM SHOREY COODEY** (1806–1849) was a mixed-blood Cherokee, whose white father raised him to understand the ways and laws of American society while growing up on his Cherokee mother's tribal land. He walked the Trail of Tears in 1838, when the Cherokee Nation was forcibly removed from southeastern US to Indian Territory, now Oklahoma. In 1839, he went on to draft and sign the Cherokee Constitution, which rejoined the Eastern and Western Cherokee into "one body politic," and he

Opposite: Congressional Cemetery chapel

Above: Nez Percé Chief Ut–Sin–Malikan Below left: Choctaw Chief Push Ma Ta Ha Below right: Chief Scarlet Crow, or Kan Ya Tu Duta, of the Sisseton-Wahpeton Oyate Band of the Eastern Sioux

became the first president of the National Committee of the Cherokee Nation.

He died of disease in DC, having come to petition Congress for memorials to the Cherokee for the Trail of Tears and reimbursement for unpaid treaty provisions. He and the other Cherokee delegates were commended by journalist Herman Viola for knowing more about US laws, institutions, and government than most members of Congress. Coodey's daughters Henrietta and Charlotte rest with him here.

Nine rows due east to the large tree and south to the next large tree stands the grand marker for Choctaw ❷ CHIEF PUSH MA TA HA (1764–1824), whose full name Apushamatahahubi means "one whose rifle, tomahawk, or bow is fatal in war or hunting." During the War of 1812, he fought alongside Major General Andrew Jackson (1767–1845), who promoted him a few times, eventually to the rank of Brigadier General by the end of the war. They became personal friends, and Push Ma Ta Ha had no fear of challenging Jackson in later years during disputed negotiations of the Treaty of Doak's Stand to reestablish boundaries of Choctaw land. He died of croup in DC on a visit to enlist Senator Jackson and President Monroe to evict white poachers settling on Choctaw land. On his deathbed, he told Jackson that he wanted a grand funeral, which his friend gave him. It was one of the largest state funerals ever held in DC, attended by Jackson, President Monroe and over 2,000 mourners.

Now make your way nine rows due east to the large tree and James Williamson's marker, then south 70 feet to the next large tree. In 1868, Nez Percé ❸ CHIEF UT-SIN-MALIKAN (1793–1868) was, by tradition, buried where he died, as a warrior for his people, rather than be repatriated by his family. He had traveled with four delegates by ship from Oregon for over four weeks to negotiate a treaty to divide tribal land again after a treaty of 1863 had shrunk tribal territory by 90%. He would also demand unpaid remuneration from previous treaties that were violated when gold was found on the land. He was plied with whiskey and refused to sign the new treaty, and was later found dead in a gutter. Members of a local women's club took care of his body and had him buried. He is said to have died by untold disease, but his family lore has it that he was pushed from his hotel window for refusing to sign the new treaty. The family's story was lost to assimilation and has only recently been heard again. A new headstone marks his head, while the original headstone lies at the foot of his grave.

Adjacent is ❹ CHIEF SCARLET CROW, or Kan Ya Tu Duta, (1825–1867) of the Sisseton-Wahpeton Oyate Band of the Eastern Sioux. He came from Dakota Territory in February 1867 to negotiate and sign a land allocation treaty with the US Government on behalf of his tribe. Two days later, unbeknownst to him, the provisions of the treaty were renegotiated, and he refused to sign. Two days after, he disappeared. After nearly three weeks, two Virginia farmers allegedly found him hanging from a tree by a piece of his wearing blanket – after the Bureau of Indian Affairs had posted a reward. Tribal delegate Joseph Brown surveyed the scene and suspected murder. He feared that others might kidnap and slay Natives in the future to collect rewards for finding them. He urged the reward not be paid, though he never pressed charges due to lack of evidence. The farmers split the $100 reward.

Now head east to the walkway and turn right, then left on Proutt Street across 14 rows, and then left at Samuel E. Little's grave. Between the graves of Lewis Yount and Charles Sonneman is the unmarked grave of Pawnee ❺ OSCAR CAREY (?–1884), a rider in *Buffalo Bill's Wild West Show*. He died of pneumonia while here intending to earn money for a farming venture. Buffalo Bill ordered his Washington agent to bury Carey "as he would accord a member of his own family." He was thus honored in accordance with Pawnee rituals by a Universalist reverend. He was buried in his full Pawnee regalia. Little else is known of him.

Return to Proutt Street and turn right. Walk past the Kingdom of Animals, uphill past family crypts and the bounty of beehives on the hillside. The DC Beekeeping Alliance manages the hives, which are home to some 1.5 million bees. The cemetery occasionally sells the honey, and the jars go fast. Now, pass Congress Street to the first graves on the fourth row to the right.

Clockwise from top left: DC Beekeeping Alliance beehives; Cherokee William Shorey Coodey; Lummi Nation's September 11 Healing Poles; Pawnee Oscar Carey (unmarked); Winnebago Chief Prophet

Above: Choctaw & Scottish Peter Pitchlynn **Below:** Matthew Brady, who photographed Native American delegations to DC

❻ **DEBORAH ANN BROKEN ROPE,** Waci Uwe, or Come Dancing, (1952–2023) was a member of the Oglala Sioux Nation and a lawyer, born and raised in DC of Native parents. She spent her life in service, most notably as an advocate and expert in Indian health, federal-Indian relations, and voting rights to the benefit of all tribes. She consulted regularly for the Bureau of Indian Affairs and the Indian Health Service, and was for a time an adjunct professor at American University. The education of Native youth was paramount for her, and she was known to have used her own resources to provide educational assistance. Her brother Frederick is buried with her.

Continue on Proutt to the ❼ **SEPTEMBER 11 HEALING POLES** that are carved from a single red cedar by the Lummi Nation's House of Tears Carvers, led by master carver Jewell Praying Wolf James. The *Liberty* pole depicts a female bear with Grandmother Moon in her abdomen, and the *Freedom* pole is a male bear with Grandfather Sun. Eagles, each with seven feathers to represent American Airlines flight 77, which hit the Pentagon, adorn each end of the Sovereignty crossbar. Peace is represented by the female eagle and war by the male.

The Lummi nations have a long tradition of creating and delivering the gift of a totem meant – via long, spiritual journeys from the Pacific Northwest – to bring attention to threats that face Indigenous communities and sacred sites, or to bring healing and hope to places affected by disaster. The Pentagon chose not to place this totem on its grounds due to security concerns. It will eventually be relocated to the 911 Memorial Grove on Kingman Island. According to one of the carvers, the totem is a gift to touch the soul, heart, and spirit, and lift one up who is crying out for help.

Walk about 50 feet past the totem, then right at the Conklyn bench, and go seven rows in to find the marker featuring an angel writing on a tablet. Scottish and Choctaw ❽ **PETER PITCHLYNN** (1806–1881) and his four children lie here. He was a drafter of the Choctaw Constitution of 1826, creator of the Choctaw national school system, Principal Chief for a time, freemason, and eminent negotiator, who fought hard for decades to get the "net proceeds" of $3 million from the US Government in payment for 10 million acres of Choctaw land ceded to Mississippi, which was only resolved years after his death. His daughter ❾ SOPHIA PITCHLYNN (1863–1942) became a chicken farmer, raising award-winning breeds. She was often noted by the Agricultural Department as a foremost expert in the field of chicken husbandry.

Walk north to Ingle Street, turn right, pass the grave of composer and conductor John Philip Sousa, and continue left on Congress Street at the chapel for about 30 feet. Turn left at William Johnson's grave. Four rows in is the grave of Winnebago ❿ CHIEF PROPHET, who came to Washington as a delegate of his tribe, the People of the First Voice, presumably to request to remain on the Blue Earth Reserve in Minnesota. The tribe fought with the British in the War of 1812, and they had been nearly annihilated by European diseases, decreasing from 25,000 to a few thousand members, who were moved five times from 1840 to 1863. Nothing is actually known of Prophet himself.

CONGRESSIONAL CEMETERY
1801 E Street SE
Washington, DC 20003
www.congressionalcemetery.org

Grave Locations:

❶ WILLIAM SHOREY COODEY
(Cherokee)
Row 43/Site 50

❷ CHIEF PUSH MA TA HA
(Choctaw)
Row 31/Site 41

❸ CHIEF UT-SIN-MALIKAN
(Nez Percé)
Row 22/Site 75

❹ CHIEF SCARLET CROW,
or Kan Ya Tu Duta (Eastern Sioux)
Row 22/Site 76

❺ OSCAR CAREY (Pawnee)
Row 6/Site 247, unmarked
To the right of Lewis C. Yount,
left of John G. Stephenson

❻ DEBORAH ANN BROKEN
ROPE, Waci Uwe, or Come Dancing
(Oglala Sioux)
Row 64/Site 263

❼ SEPTEMBER 11 HEALING
POLES (Lummi)
Proutt Street & September 11
Memorial pathway

❽ PETER PITCHLYNN (Choctaw)
Row 87/Site 294

❾ SOPHIA PITCHLYNN
(Choctaw)
Row 88/Site 294

❿ CHIEF PROPHET
(Winnebago)
Row 63/Site 147

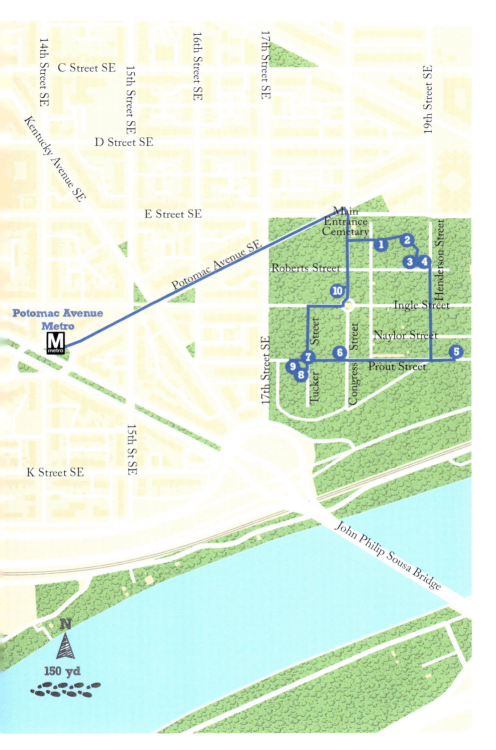

17 Nouveau Riche & Strivers Walk

Gilded Age excess coexisting with Black excellence

> **BEST TIME:** Any season or time of day
> **DISTANCE:** Approximately 2 miles
> **ROUTE DESCRIPTION:** Flat with plenty of eye candy for architecture and history buffs
> **START:** Metro at Dupont Circle (Red Line)
> **END:** Metro at Dupont Circle (Red Line)

Dupont Circle has been a bastion for heiresses and nouveau-riche socialites, the epicenter of Gay Rights activism, and home to Black intellectuals and elites. The south side of the circle was once the border of habitable DC. The area was muddy countryside with putrid air wafting from a slaughterhouse. It became a brickyard and a shantytown, until DC Governor Alexander "Boss" Shepard (1835–1902) and the "California Syndicate" of mine owners initiated development activities. Doyennes hosted lavish parties with the most sought-after invitations. Urban lore tells of spies, trysts, and bitter feuds, as the wealthy placed themselves close to the nation's political center. The 1929 Stock Market crash was not kind to these residents, and nearly all sold off their mansions, which became diplomatic outposts, clubhouses, and unusual museums.

At the Q Street entrance to the Dupont Circle Metro station, you'll find a poem etched into the wall above the escalators, excerpted from Walt Whitman's "The Wound Dresser". A second excerpt from "We Embrace" by DC poet E. Ethelbert Miller encompasses a circular bench 180 degrees behind the escalator. Together, these two spots comprise the ❶ **HIV/AIDS CAREGIVERS MEMORIAL** to honor those who steadfastly nursed their partners and friends through the devastating health crisis.

Opposite: First Daughter Alice Roosevelt Longworth's House

Above: Colombian Ambassador's Residence, or, Thomas T. Gaff House

Turning back, look west across 20th Street to the ❷ **COLOMBIAN AMBASSADOR'S RESIDENCE,** originally built by Thomas T. Gaff, a wealthy businessman. This 1905 stunner was inspired by the 17th-century Château Balleroy in Normandy, France. It was known for its state-of-the-art amenities like a cork-insulated wine cellar, a trap door to the icehouse to enable delivery from the street, a hot-air system for drying clothes, and its Edwardian ballroom.

To the right on 20th Street, follow your nose to ❸ **ZORBA'S CAFÉ,** a family-owned Greek eatery serving the neighborhood since 1984, named for the title character in the novel and film *Zorba the Greek*. Back in the day, the patriarch would sit down with his guests to chat over a glass of red wine or retsina. Now head back down 20th Street NW for one block, and turn right onto Massachusetts Avenue.

"If you haven't got anything nice to say about anyone, come sit next to me." Alice Roosevelt, daughter of President Theodore Roosevelt, had this phrase embroidered on a pillow adorning a settee in her upstairs sitting room in ❹ ALICE ROOSEVELT LONGWORTH HOUSE. She was an author, socialite, hellion, and the first White House "wild child," not to mention the sharpest wit with the sharpest of tongues. Her father once said, "I can either run the country or I can attend to Alice, but I cannot possibly do both."

Look across the avenue towards the ❺ EMBASSY OF INDONESIA in the former Walsh-McClean House. This extravagant home was built in 1903 for a sultan's ransom of $835,000 ($29 million today), making it the costliest home in the city in its day. A once penniless, Irish carpenter, Thomas Walsh (1850–1910) struck gold in Colorado, yielding him $3 million ($105 million today). He moved with his wife and daughter Evalyn (1886–1947) to DC to be close to power. They flowed easily into the social scene, hosting grand fêtes, with handmade, gold flatware from his Camp Bird mine always adorning the dining table. Evalyn later owned the Hope Diamond, the largest blue diamond ever cut, and she wore it as everyday jewelry. Today, the diamond is on view at the Smithsonian Institution's National Museum of Natural History. The mansion was purchased in 1951 for a relative song to become the Embassy of Indonesia. Saraswati, the Hindu Goddess of learning and wisdom, graces its entrance.

Continue right and pause to admire the ❻ MAHATMA GANDHI STATUE, a gift from the people of India, poised as if striding to his next destination.

Up a block, look across to see ❼ THE SOCIETY OF THE CINCINNATI, founded in 1783. Outfitted with a no-holds-barred budget, American diplomat Larz Anderson (1866–1937) and his author wife Isabel (1876–1948) built their mansion in 1905 with the most modern amenities – telephone, electricity, central heating, and two elevators. They left their estate as a museum and clubhouse to his beloved institution. Members of The Society of the Cincinnati are male descendants of commissioned officers of the Continental Army and Navy, and their French counterparts as well. They regularly host public tours, concerts, and events.

On your right, the ornate, private ❽ COSMOS CLUB is one of the city's pillars of scientific and intellectual fellowship, founded in 1871. The Philosophical Society of Washington is also in residence here. Founded in 1877 with the first secretary of the Smithsonian, Joseph Henry, as its first president, the society meets regularly, and the public is invited to join in the dialogue to promote scientific education. The mansion itself was rebuilt by railroad and coal heiress and socialite Mary Scott Townsend (1854–1931) from what was the home of "California Syndicate" investor Curtis J. Hillyer (1828–1906), and later sold to the Cosmos Club. The rather clandestine Syndicate, led by Nevada Senator William Morris Stewart, purchased undeveloped land, subdivided it into tracts upon which were built many Gilded Age mansions. In keeping with the grandeur of the neighbors, elaborate, Beaux Arts embellishments adorn the Louis XVI-inspired exterior. The public may tour the mansion six times per year with a special reservation.

Turn right on Florida Avenue and right on Hillyer Court to reach the intimate ❾ IA&A AT HILLYER gallery, part of the International Art & Artists program that engenders cross-cultural exchange and insight through contemporary art, often in collaboration with embassies and cultural organizations.

Two blocks on, on your left is the lovely ❿ FRIENDS MEETING HOUSE, or Quaker House, established in 1930, with Lou Henry Hoover (1874–1944) present for the laying of the cornerstone. She and her husband President Herbert Hoover (1874–1964) were regular worshippers here. The Pennsylvania Foxcroft stone is uncommon and no longer available, perhaps symbolically, from the land where Quakers were first established in the US. In spring, the grounds are absolutely resplendent with flowers and greenery.

Continue right up Florida Avenue, to the ⓫ AMERICAN GEOPHYSICAL UNION, whose mission is to "inspire, educate, and empower the next generation of scientists in order to sustain discovery and solution-based research." You can pre-book a tour of this net-zero-energy building and discover the key principles of its sus-

Clockwise from top left: Henry's Soul Cafe; sidewalk solar system of American Geophysical Union; poem for HIV/AIDS Caregiver Memorial at Dupont Circle station; Saraswati, Hindu Goddess of Wisdom and Learning

tainability. Inside, look at the floors made of ground up toilets and sinks and the themes of space, air, land and oceans. Do you see the scaled solar system of marble and brass embedded in the sidewalk?

One block beyond the AGU, turn right on T Street NW and continue to the next block, to the petite 🔵 **MUSEUM OF THE PALESTINIAN PEOPLE** on your left. It opened in 2019 and focuses on celebrating and preserving Palestinian art, culture, and history. By

Above: Second Empire row houses owned by Frederick Douglass' family

now a margarita is surely in order. Diagonally across the street is ⓭ LAURIOL PLAZA, a neighborhood anchor for great cocktails, bountiful good Mexican eats, and gracious service, since 1983.

The next block is part of the roughly 10-square-block Strivers' Section, once known as the community of Black aristocracy. From the 1870s through the mid-1900s, prior to and after to the influx of the nouveaux riches, this part of the city was home to influential Black entrepreneurs, educators, scientists, authors, architects, politicians, and civil servants. Among the neighborhood luminaries were activist Mary Church Terrell and poet Langston Hughes.

Prominent architects contributed to the aesthetic here with simple, rhythmically repeating-design row houses, which fit in with the styles of the surrounding mansions as the area grew. "Strivers" was a common, once disparaging term for African Americans who bought houses from white owners. To pioneering Black Americans, though, it meant, "We arrived" and became a positive title for those moving beyond segregated neighborhoods into new ones around the city.

The charming ⓮ ITALIANATE ROW HOUSES at 1764–1778 T Street NW are among the oldest residences in the section. At the end of the block was the home of ⓯ TODD DUNCAN, George Gershwin's personal choice to premier the title role in *Porgy and Bess* on Broadway in 1935, a role he went on to play some 1,800 times – except in DC's segregated National Theatre. He later became a Howard University vocal instructor.

Amble your way north on 17th Street to the intersection with U Street NW. Across U Street at the far edge of the section are three buildings of note. Abolitionist, publisher, and oft called "Father of the Civil Rights Movement" Frederick Douglass bought the ⓰ SECOND EMPIRE-STYLE ROW HOUSES at 2000–2004 17th Street NW in 1875 as a financial investment that enabled him to live his last 20 years in his beloved mansion in Anacostia. His heirs owned this row until 1965.

Back across U Street, order treats for later at ⓱ HENRY'S SOUL CAFE, a family-owned, soul-food carryout that has been serving their noteworthy sweet potato pie and comfort food on this corner since 1968.

Double back five blocks on 17th Street NW and turn left on S Street NW to the middle of the block to the home of ⓲ MARY CHURCH TERRELL (1863–1954), civil rights activist, agitator, educator, author, and co-founder of the NAACP. She is also know as the primary force behind the legislation that in 1953 ended segregation in DC restaurants. She paid a premium for this row house in 1924, as the owners did not want to sell it to a woman of color, and she lived there for 30 years enjoying the company of DC's intelligentsia until her death.

Walk back two blocks to where Harlem Renaissance author ⓳ LANGSTON HUGHES (1902–1967) lived on and off with his mother and brother on the unheated second floor of this row house, all the while writing many poems inspired by spirituals and blues. One day at work as a busboy, he mustered the nerve to show three poems to poet Vachel Lindsay (1879–1931), who read them and commented to reporters, "I just met a busboy poet." This was the spark that lit the way to Hughes' illustrious career. His subsequent prolific writings on the life of working-class Blacks earned him both revulsion and admiration throughout his career.

❶ HIV/AIDS CAREGIVERS MEMORIAL
Dupont Circle Metro Station Q & 20th Street NW entrance
Washington, DC 20009

❷ COLOMBIAN AMBASSADOR'S RESIDENCE
1520 20th Street NW
Washington, DC 20009

❸ ZORBA'S CAFÉ
1612 20th Street NW
Washington, DC 20009
www.zorbascafedc.com

❹ ALICE ROOSEVELT LONGWORTH HOUSE
2009 Massachusetts Avenue NW
Washington, DC 20036

❺ EMBASSY OF INDONESIA / FORMER WALSH-MCCLEAN HOUSE
2020 Massachusetts Avenue NW
Washington, DC 20036
www.kemlu.go.id/washington/en

❻ MAHATMA GANDHI STATUE
Massachusetts Avenue & 21st Street NW
Washington, DC 20036

❼ THE SOCIETY OF THE CINCINNATI
2118 Massachusetts Avenue NW
Washington, DC 20008
www.societyofthecincinnati.org

❽ COSMOS CLUB
2121 Massachusetts Avenue NW
Washington, DC 20008
www.cosmosclub.org/activities/visiting-the-club/mansion-tours

❾ IA&A AT HILLYER
9 Hillyer Court NW
Washington, DC 20008
www.athillyer.org

❿ FRIENDS MEETING HOUSE
2111 Decatur Place NW
Washington, DC 20008
www.quakersdc.org/about

⓫ AMERICAN GEOPHYSICAL UNION
2000 Florida Avenue NW
Washington, DC 20009
www.agu.org/building/pages/tour

⓬ MUSEUM OF THE PALESTINIAN PEOPLE
1900 18th Street NW
Washington, DC 20009
www.mpp-dc.org

⓭ LAURIOL PLAZA
1835 18th Street NW
Washington, DC 20009
www.lauriolplaza.com

⓮ ITALIANATE ROW HOUSES
1764–1778 T Street NW
Washington, DC 20009

⓯ TODD DUNCAN HOUSE
1700 T Street NW
Washington, DC 20009

⓰ SECOND EMPIRE-STYLE ROW HOUSES
2000–2004 17th Street NW
Washington, DC 20009

⓱ HENRY'S SOUL CAFÉ
1704 U Street NW
Washington, DC 20009
www.henryssoulcafe.com

⓲ MARY CHURCH TERRELL HOUSE
1615 S Street NW
Washington, DC 20009

⓳ LANGSTON HUGHES HOUSE
1749 S Street NW
Washington, DC 20009

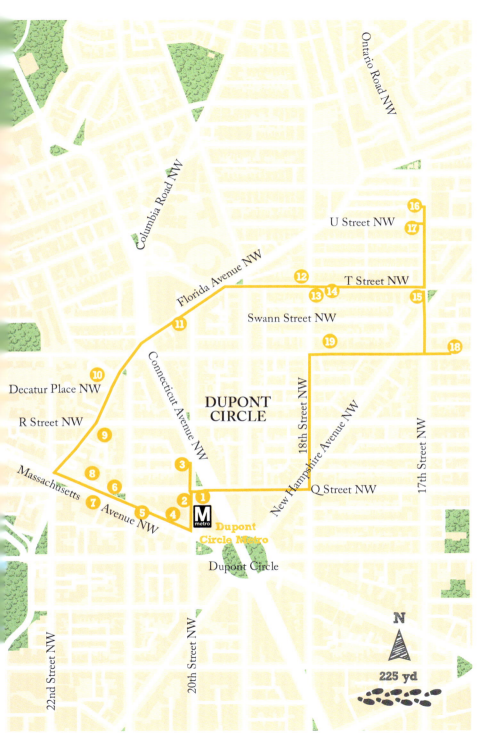

POTOMAC RIVER NW & SW

18 __ Riverfront Walk
Lore of the Nation's River

> **BEST TIME:** Especially nice in spring and winter, with and without leaves on trees
> **DISTANCE:** Approximately 3.3 miles
> **ROUTE DESCRIPTION:** Mostly flat
> **START:** Metro at Foggy Bottom (Blue, Orange, Silver Lines)
> **END:** Metro at Smithsonian (Blue, Orange, Silver Lines)

The Potomac River is considered DC's lifeblood and was once one of the major transportation routes of the new nation. It flows with history.

The river is three million years old, with its origin 173 miles north in West Virginia. It flows about 400 miles to the mouth of the Chesapeake Bay, dropping over 3,000 feet in altitude along the way. Indigenous people first lived along the river around 14,000 years ago, and the name originates from a Patawomeck village near the mouth of the bay, but the meaning remains unclear due to its now lost language origin. British Captain John Smith (1580–1631) and his crew were the first Europeans to explore the Chesapeake Bay and the river, though Spanish and French explorers knew of them 90 years prior. Smith incorporated surprisingly accurate details into his 1612 map of Virginia, including Indigenous villages throughout the region.

From 1751, Georgetown was an established tobacco trading port. In 1791, George Washington selected the area as a strategic location for the capital of the fledgling country. Over generations, the riverfront has played many different roles. It's been a manufacturing and distribution place for armaments; host to cotton, flour and paper mills, breweries, nightclubs, and a glass plant. Water sports and recreation have a long tradition on the river too.

Washington spent much of his career surveying the Potomac region and knew the value of expanding transportation routes, connecting tra-

Opposite: Kayakers on the Potomac River

Above: *Scarlet Natural Chaos* sculpture

de to the Forks of the Ohio in present day Pittsburgh. He founded the Potomac Company in 1785 to do just that. By 1858, the Chesapeake and Ohio (C&O) Canal was finally complete and already obsolete, overshadowed by the speed and capacity of the transcontinental railroad. Your walk begins here at canal ❶ **LOCK 3,** where you can see the replica of a 19th-century barge, once pulled by mules along towpaths on either side of the canal. From April or May through late October, costumed guides give enlightening tours aboard the barge, painting a timeline of canal life as you lumber half a mile through Lock 3, one of the few remaining of the original 74 locks. The mechanics of it are impressive.

The ❷ **BUST OF SUPREME COURT JUSTICE WILLIAM O. DOUGLASS** (1898–1980) tributes the man credited with saving the canal. After inviting several congressmen for a walk on a nearby trail, he convinced Congress to declare it a National Park. Five percent of all historic structures within the entire National Park System are in the 184.5-mile-long C&O Canal National Park, including rustic lock houses to rent.

Head right to 31st Street. Diagonally across is the former site of ❸ **HOLLERITH'S TABULATING MACHINE COMPANY,** where Herman Hollerith (1860–1929) invented the punch card tabulating machine, first used to conduct the 1890 Census and a significant precursor of the electronic computer.

Walk left on 31st Street to the river. The ❹ *MOTHER EARTH SCULPTURE,* a symbol of global sustainability and call to action against climate change, is sculpted by Barton Rubenstein, local co-founder of the Mother Earth Project. One of several like sculptures in major global cities, *Mother Earth* faces downriver towards the world's oceans, "a body of water connecting all nations," according to the artist.

Go left along the Georgetown Waterfront Park boardwalk, noting the ❺ **HYDRAULIC FLOODGATES** built to protect the Washington Harbour complex from getting inundated when floodwaters rise 7 to 12 feet. The worst flooding to date neared 18 feet in 1942. The 57 gates were state of the art in 1986 when they were installed. They have only been used some 12 times since then, and they have epically failed more than once.

At the east end of the complex stands ❻ *SCARLET NATURAL CHAOS* by Arnie Quinz. This ode to femininity and the scarlet oak, DC's official tree, is rooted in the history of the city. As the artist says, it is "a statement on modern culture's loss of connection with nature."

Opposite is the patently Scandinavian ❼ **HOUSE OF SWEDEN,** home to the Embassies of Sweden, Iceland, and Liechtenstein. The Swedes are famously hospitable, offering a bounty of public events indoors, in their gallery, and on the stunning rooftop overlooking the water.

Just to the right is a giant non-working ❽ **SUNDIAL.** Its origins are unknown, and yet it piques curiosity. By design and with precise placement, sundials display accurate local solar time, and when used with a sextant or octant, they can precisely determine location on earth or on water. Before the advent of modern navigational technology, sailors and navigators used the position of the sun to determine their location at sea.

Walk a little further along the path to find a Park Service plaque on the left where the ❾ **HERRING HIGHWAY** begins. This is the route that herring and alewife swim in early spring as they make their way from the Atlantic Ocean to the Chesapeake Bay, up the Potomac River, and into Rock Creek to spawn. They then turn around and swim back the way they came.

To the right, downriver of Thompson's Boat House, is the ❿ **MILE 0 MARKER** of the C&O Canal towpath, the mouth of Rock Creek, and the Washington City Canal Outfall.

Come back to cross the bridge over Rock Creek and Virginia Avenue NW to the ⓫ **WATERGATE COMPLEX & HOTEL.** The mixed residential and business complex was made notorious by a presidential scandal in 1972, but it began with an architectural scandal. Italian architect Luigi Moretti (1907–1973) insisted that the residential, hotel, and commercial complex be built as designed, though it infringed on zoning regulations and height restrictions. After several years of negotiations with local powers that be, the structure was completed and opened in 1965 to much fanfare. A tour of the Watergate Scandal Suite, decorated with nods to the 1972 ordeal, can be arranged with the hotel concierge, or you can book a stay in it.

Now continue right along the Parkway path. Before there was ⓬ **JOHN F. KENNEDY CENTER FOR THE PERFORMING ARTS,** there was the venerable Christian Heurich Brewing Company on this site. Heurich (1842–1945), orphaned as an adolescent, worked his way through Germany learning the brewing trade and arrived in DC with a few dollars in his pocket. He began his first commercial brewery in Foggy Bottom, which suffered through two destructive fires and a long drought due to Prohibition, during which he sold ice to stay afloat. This site was his third brewery, designed to be fireproof. The company survived until 1956 and was razed in 1962. His recipes are now brewed by two DC breweries.

Senator John Kennedy (1917–1963) and his wife Jackie (1929–1994) were stellar fundraisers in the effort to build a national performing arts center with six different stages. Upon its opening in 1971,

Clockwise from top left: John Quincy Adams swimming spot; Kennedy Center riverside terrace; Justice William O. Douglas bust; *Milk River* sculpture; cakes and coffee; *Mother Earth* sculpture

Above: Theodore Roosevelt Island in the foreground from the roof of the Kennedy Center Below: Zero Milestone marker of Rock Creek

it was named as a living memorial in JFK's honor. Enter through the Hall of States, where flags of all states, DC, and protectorates hang in order of admission to the union. You can go up to the airy roof terrace to take in the expansive view of the Potomac. In the background and to the right is the Healy Hall spire of Georgetown University and the National Cathedral. You'll also see ❸ **THEODORE ROOSEVELT ISLAND,** where General John Mason (1766–1849) built his summer Analostan plantation. It was then used as a training ground for the Civil War US Colored Troops. Today, it is a living presidential memorial park to the original Rough Rider, who gave us the National Parks System.

Exit the Kennedy Center to the right towards ❹ **THE REACH,** the multi-functional addition to the center, which opened in 2019. You'll find creative and cultural programming here, including rehearsals, children's activities, outdoor movie projections, and much more. Be sure to take a turn around the garden to admire its lovely sculptures and plantings, grab a drink for the road, and then follow the pedestrian bridge to the riverside.

Walk, then fork left, passing the newly modernized volleyball courts on the right. Wind around to the imposing steps that seem to have no raison d'être other than being the bane of runners' existence. In the L'Enfant city plan, there was to be an entrance to the city from the river with these grand ❺ **WATERGATE STEPS** as the gateway. Though that never materialized, the National Symphony Orchestra made jubilant use of this unique venue from 1935 to 1965, playing concerts on specially designed band shell barges docked at the river's edge, while music lovers sat on the steps. President Franklin Roosevelt (1882–1945) turned up on opening night and watched from the comfort of his limousine parked on the roadway. Unfortunately, the disruptive jet noise coming from National Airport, along with safety issues due to increased jet traffic, led to the end of the concerts.

Pass under ❻ **ARLINGTON MEMORIAL BRIDGE,** which connects DC and Arlington, Virginia in a symbolic, post-Civil War reconciliation. Look closely at the bridge's architectural majesty and emblems along its piers.

⑰ **JOHN QUINCY ADAMS** (1767–1848) visited a favorite swimming spot in the river as part of his daily, two-hour routine during his tenure in DC. He arose before dawn, walked to the river, went for an hour-long swim, and walked home. In cold weather, he walked two miles around the city each day, foregoing an icy swim. On a few occasions, the tide nearly washed away the president's clothes. Though his exact trajectory is unknown, we can assume that the spot near Independence Avenue, once Tiber Creek, is a likely one.

Where you now see softball fields to the left was once the site of the ⑱ **NATIONAL POLO GROUNDS,** where Sunday matches were a fun and uncommon sports spectacle along the river. The polo clubs left this field in 1999.

Within the mini traffic circle is the ⑲ **CAPTAIN JOHN ERICSSON MEMORIAL,** an elegant tribute to the Swedish engineer and inventor (1803–1889), whose design of the iron-clad *USS Monitor* changed the course of maritime warfare during the Civil War and aided in preserving US Naval supremacy. His most notable invention was the screw propeller that revolutionized naval propulsion, and his numerous maritime inventions and research in solar energy all still serve us today.

With the river at your right, continue to a stone, adjacent to ball field #3, with the ⑳ **FIRST AIR MAIL FLIGHT MARKER,** where Lt. George Boyle flew the first, though ill-fated, flight for Philadelphia in 1918 in a Curtiss Jenny biplane of the upside-down stamp fame. Thus began the continuously scheduled air mail service between DC, Philadelphia, and New York City.

Continue along Ohio Drive to the ㉑ **OHIO DRIVE BRIDGE,** part of the flood-control system of the Tidal Basin. Look for the fishlike gargoyles, which are caricatures created by the beloved and longserving regional director of the National Park Service Manus "Jack" Fish (1928–2010). They were added on after the bridge's construction.

Keep walking to the fork and go right to Parking Lot A. As the Spanish inscription states, the ㉒ **CUBAN AMERICAN FRIENDSHIP URN** is carved from the remains of a hurricane-damaged me-

Above: Tidal Basin through the lens of the Ohio Drive Bridge
Below: Inventor Captain John Ericsson Memorial

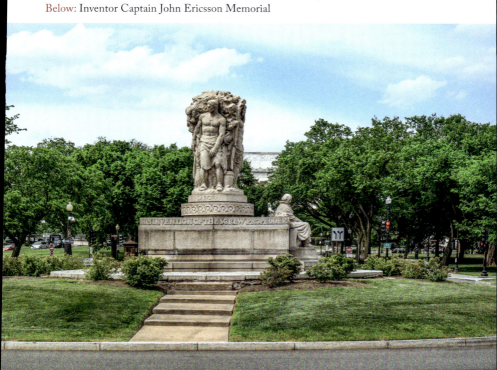

Clockwise from top left: George Mason Memorial; C&O Canal barge guide; First Airmail Flight marker; Thompson Boat Center

morial to the victims of the *USS Maine,* which exploded in the Havana Harbor and sparked the Spanish American War in 1898. Clasped hands of the US and Cuba symbolize the friendship between the nations in the aftermath of the war.

From this serene spot, double back and turn right at the fork to the ㉓ **GEORGE MASON MEMORIAL,** a delightful garden and memorial in any weather to the man who authored the Virginia Declaration of Rights, a major influence on Thomas Jefferson's writing of the US Declaration of Independence. The memorial is sculpted by local artist Wendy M. Ross.

Continue sauntering along at your leisure and see what other riverside sites you can locate. In springtime this walk is an explosion of cherry blossoms and flowers.

❶ LOCK 3
C&O Canal
at Thomas Jefferson Street NW
Washington, DC 20007
www.nps.gov/choh/index.htm

❷ BUST OF SUPREME COURT JUSTICE WILLIAM O. DOUGLASS
C&O Canal at Thomas
Jefferson Street NW
Washington, DC 20007

❸ HOLLERITH'S TABULATING MACHINE COMPANY
1054 31st Street NW
Washington, DC 20007

❹ *MOTHER EARTH* SCULPTURE
Friends of Georgetown Park,
at west end of boardwalk
Washington, DC 20007
www.motherearthproject.org/mother-earth-sculptures

❺ HYDRAULIC FLOODGATES
Washington Harbour
3000 K Street NW
Washington, DC 20007

❻ *SCARLET NATURAL CHAOS*
30th Street & Potomac River
Washington, DC 20007
www.arnequinze.com/art-and-exhibitions/scarlet-natural-chaos

❼ HOUSE OF SWEDEN
2900 K Street NW
Washington, DC 20007
www.houseofsweden.com/about

❽ SUNDIAL
30th Street & Potomac River
Washington, DC 20007

❾ HERRING HIGHWAY
30th Street & Potomac River
Path adjacent to sundial
Washington, DC 20037

POTOMAC RIVER NW & SW

❿ MILE 0 MARKER
Virginia Avenue NW & Rock Creek
beyond Thompson's Boat House
Washington, DC 20037
www.canaltrust.org/pyv/
mile-marker-0-0tide-lock

⓫ WATERGATE COMPLEX & HOTEL
2650 Virginia Avenue NW
Washington, DC 20037

⓬ JOHN F. KENNEDY CENTER FOR THE PERFORMING ARTS/ CHRISTIAN HEURICH BREWING COMPANY
2700 F Street NW
Washington, DC 20566
www.kennedy-center.org

⓭ THEODORE ROOSEVELT ISLAND
Middle of Potomac River
View from the rooftop
of Kennedy Center

⓮ THE REACH
2700 F Street NW
Washington, DC 20566
www.kennedy-center.org/visit

⓯ WATERGATE STEPS
Lincoln Memorial Circle
at Rock Creek Parkway
Washington, DC 20004

⓰ ARLINGTON MEMORIAL BRIDGE
Memorial Bridge
at Rock Creek Parkway
Washington, DC 20004
www.nps.gov/gwmp/planyourvisit/
memorialave.htm

⓱ JOHN QUINCY ADAMS SWIMMING SPOT
Ohio Drive & Independence Avenue
& 23rd Street SW
Washington, DC 20004

⓲ NATIONAL POLO GROUNDS
West Potomac Park
Ohio Drive & Independence
Avenue SW
Washington, DC 20004

⓳ CAPTAIN JOHN ERICSSON MEMORIAL
Ohio Drive & Independence
Avenue & 23rd Street SW
Washington, DC 20004
www.nps.gov/nama/planyourvisit/
john-ericsson-memorial.htm

⓴ FIRST AIR MAIL FLIGHT MARKER
West Potomac Park
Ohio Drive adjacent to baseball field #3
Washington, DC 20024
www.nps.gov/places/000/
first-air-mail-marker.htm

㉑ OHIO DRIVE BRIDGE
Ohio Drive at Tidal Basin
Washington, DC 20004

㉒ CUBAN AMERICAN FRIENDSHIP URN
971 Ohio Drive SW
Washington, DC 20024
www.nps.gov/places/000/
cuban-american-friendship-urn.htm

㉓ GEORGE MASON MEMORIAL
East Basin & Ohio Drives SW
Washington, DC 20024
www.nps.gov/nama/planyourvisit/
george-mason-memorial.htm

NATIONAL MALL | DOWNTOWN DC NW

19 __ Secret Gardens Walk

Charming outdoor spaces and quiet oases

> BEST TIME: Best during spring, summer, and fall
> DISTANCE: 1.4 miles
> ROUTE DESCRIPTION: Flat on tree-lined sidewalks that can be crowded at times
> START: Metro at Federal Triangle (Blue, Orange, Silver Lines)
> END: Metro at Union Station (Red Line)

When the day's destination is the National Mall, most people head directly for the monuments, memorials, and museums. Though it's also known as "America's Front Yard," most people are surprised to learn that it's surrounded by several "secret" gardens designed to enhance the overall museum experience even further.

Across the Mall is the Smithsonian's demonstration vegetable garden, a ❶ MODERN VICTORY GARDEN on the east side of the National Museum of American History. In 1944, about 20 million Victory Gardens provided 8 million tons of food, roughly 40 percent of all the produce consumed in the United States that year. These home-based vegetable gardens allowed businesses to focus their efforts on getting food to the troops overseas. The Smithsonian's World War II–era garden was designed based on a 1943 pamphlet. All of the plants here are heirlooms from the 1940s, and some even date back to before Shakespeare's time.

During his presidency, Abraham Lincoln established the US Department of Agriculture (USDA) in 1862. He described it as "The People's Department." So it was fitting that the ❷ PEOPLE'S GARDEN was created on February 12, 2009 to commemorate Lincoln's 200th birthday. Its purpose is to educate the public about growing nutritious food, and sustainable gardening practices. All of the produce grown here is donated to the local community. At Indepen-

Opposite: Enid A. Haupt Garden

Clockwise from top left: National Museum of the American Indian; flowers in the People's Garden; Summerhouse; fountain; Victory Garden

dence Avenue and 14th Street SW, the USDA hosts a farmers market on Fridays from May to October, offering fresh produce, cooking demonstrations, and live entertainment.

Head back toward Jefferson Drive SW and the ❸ **THE CASTLE,** which is the Smithsonian Institution Building. The Castle was the organization's first building. Founding donor James Smithson (1765–1829), an English chemist and mineralogist, left $500,000 ($16,351,000 in today's dollars) in his will to establish the institution that also bears his name. He had never visited the United States while alive, but his remains were moved to the Castle in 1905. Today, you can visit Smithson's crypt inside the north entrance of the Castle.

At the corner of the Castle, turn right and follow the path. Facing Independence Avenue SW on the other side of the Castle is another colorful garden oasis. The ❹ **ENID A. HAUPT GARDEN** was designed to be a modern representation of American Victorian gardens as they appeared in the mid to late 19th century. It has three sections: a Moon Gate garden inspired by a 15th-century Chinese temple in Beijing; a Victorian-style parterre garden; and a Moorish-style garden with a mosaic fountain modeled after ones in the Alhambra in Granada, Spain. Few visitors know that this is actually a rooftop garden, as it rests on the roofs of the underground African Art Museum, the Sackler Gallery, and the S. Dillon Ripley Center, which is a meeting, exhibition, and office space.

Located near the African Art Museum is the ❺ **ANDREW JACKSON DOWNING URN.** In the middle of the 19th century, Downing (1815–1852) helped steer American popular taste in landscape and garden design toward more natural, picturesque modes. In 1850, he transformed the Mall into the nation's first landscaped public park.

Located on the other side of 4th Street SW, the extensive landscape surrounding the undulating ❻ **NATIONAL MUSEUM OF THE AMERICAN INDIAN** honors North America's Indigenous lands prior to European colonization. There are naturalistic wetlands, a hardwood forest, a meadow, an immense waterfall, and croplands. There are

40 large "Grandfather Rocks," which are boulders that represent respect for the land, and four cardinal direction markers that pay tribute to Native Peoples of the North, South, East, and West.

From here, head to the US Botanic Garden. At 3rd Street SW, turn right and walk to Maryland Avenue SW. The US Botanic Garden is the oldest continuously operating garden in the country and home to over 100,000 plant specimens, many of them rare. As you explore the grounds, venture to the ● **FIRST LADIES WATER GARDEN**, located on the far side of the building. The fountain is the only memorial that recognizes American First Ladies. The granite design of the fountain is based on the classic colonial quilt pattern used by Martha Washington at her Mount Vernon home. The water garden was inaugurated in a special ceremony in 2006 by First Lady Laura Bush.

Exit the Botanic Garden at Independence Avenue SW and cross the avenue to the ● **BARTHOLDI FOUNTAIN AND GARDENS**. Many people don't realize this green space has been a part of the Botanic Garden campus since 1932. The centerpiece of the garden is the Fountain of Light and Water, more commonly known as the Bartholdi Fountain, named after French sculptor and painter Frédéric Auguste Bartholdi (1834–1904), best known for designing the Statue of Liberty.

Bartholdi hoped to sell duplicates of the elegant fountain to help finance completion of the Statue of Liberty. But buyers weren't very interested until famed landscape architect Frederick Law Olmsted (1822–1093), who was redesigning the Capitol Grounds at the time, got involved. The US Government paid $6,000 for the fountain, which was about half of its estimated value. The fountain became the Botanic Garden's centerpiece and a city landmark.

Cross the entire length of the Mall side of the US Capitol and fork right onto Northwest Drive. When visiting the Capitol, one of the bigger surprises you'll find is the ● **SUMMERHOUSE**, a squat, red-brick building on the Capitol grounds between First Street NW

Opposite: First Ladies Water Garden

and New Jersey Avenue NW that you'll see on your right. Look for a fountain in the middle, seats around the side, and a grotto. Inside the Summerhouse, seating for 22 people provides an ample area to rest and relax. In the center, a fountain provides a calming atmosphere.

Completed in late 1880 or early 1881, it was created by Olmsted in response to complaints that visitors to the Capitol could not find water or a place to rest on their journey. The fountain originally provided water for visitors and their horses, and today there are drinking fountains. Olmstead wanted to make the structure close enough to the Capitol without intruding upon its grandeur, but he also wanted to make sure there was enough foot traffic to keep it from being used for "improper purposes." It is open in the spring and summer during daylight hours.

❶ MODERN VICTORY GARDEN
1200 Constitution Avenue NW
Washington, DC 20560
www.gardens.si.edu

❷ PEOPLE'S GARDEN
(US Department of Agriculture)
1400 Independence Avenue SW
Washington, DC 20560
www.usda.gov/peoples-garden

❸ THE CASTLE
Smithsonian Institution Building
1000 Jefferson Drive SW
Washington, DC 20560
www.si.edu/museums/
smithsonian-institution-building

❹ ENID A. HAUPT GARDEN
1050 Independence Avenue SW
Washington, DC 20560
www.gardens.si.edu/gardens/
haupt-garden/

❺ ANDREW JACKSON
DOWNING URN
1050 Independence Avenue SW
Washington, DC 20560

❻ NATIONAL MUSEUM
OF THE AMERICAN INDIAN
4th Street & Independence Avenue SW
Washington, DC 20560
www.americanindian.si.edu

❼ FIRST LADIES
WATER GARDEN
US Botanic Garden
100 Maryland Avenue SW
Washington, DC 20560
www.usbg.gov

❽ BARTHOLDI
FOUNTAIN & GARDENS
US Botanic Garden
245 First Street SW
Washington, DC 20024
www.usbg.gov/gardens-plants/
bartholdi-fountain-and-gardens

❾ SUMMERHOUSE
East Capital Circle
US Capitol Grounds
Washington, DC 20004
www.aoc.gov/explore-capitol-campus/
buildings-grounds/capitol-building/
capitol-grounds/summerhouse

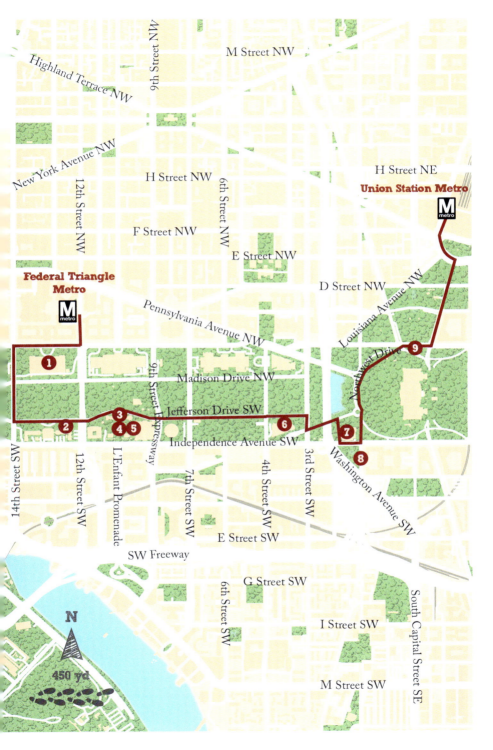

CONGRESS HEIGHTS SE

20 Soul of the City Walk
Proud entrepreneurs and grand restorations prevail

> **BEST TIME:** Daytime for walking and nighttime for events
> **DISTANCE:** Approximately 1.1 miles
> **ROUTE DESCRIPTION:** Flat, stay alert for an array of architecture and street art
> **START:** Metro at Congress Heights (Green Line)
> **END:** Metro at Congress Heights (Green Line)

Congress Heights was originally dubbed the Soul of the City for a promotional campaign, and these words resonate intensely when you stop to chat with local business owners and entrepreneurs. The economy of the neighborhood was largely driven by St. Elizabeth's Hospital, known as St. E's, a large mental institution until 2003. Today, it has been consolidated to its West Campus, and the rest of the campus is being reconfigured for government agencies, housing, business development, and public event venues.

The public sections are mostly on the East Campus, which is where this walk takes you. The architectural innovation and landscape design, much of which is on historic registers, is notable and quite a visual treat to explore.

A local creative entrepreneur named Reek says, "Congress Heights is one of the only neighborhoods in DC that still feels like where we grew up. It looks the same and has the same energy, and it is where native Washingtonians stand taller." Most of the small businesses are owned by the original proprietor or a member of the family and have served the neighborhood for decades.

Here, your Congress Heights visit starts with the bright pink ❶ **CHERRY BLOSSOM FENCE MURAL,** a trademark image of artist Chris Pyrate serving as a connector from Metro buses to the neighborhood. It is Pyrate's tribute to the people he has lost to vio-

Opposite: Cherry Blossom mural by Chris Pyrate

Above: R.I.S.E Demonstration Center Below left: Cherry Blossom seat, part of a citywide art campaign Below right: The Museum DC streetwear shop

lence and to the city's cherished blooms. Adjacent ❷ SYCAMORE & OAK RETAIL VILLAGE is a business incubator that hosts Black-owned fashion initiatives and other lifestyle businesses, as well as public events. Look for the unique, eco-wooden pavilion, known by locals as the "tree house," that stands out as a nod to modern green architecture among the historic brick buildings of this section of the former Saint Elizabeth's Hospital campus. A small food emporium here serves coffee, food, and cocktails with names like "Mayor for Life." Try the drool-worthy crab fries. Many of the business owners live in or have roots in Congress Heights, and all are deeply bonded to the community. Go-go is the dominant sound here.

The anchor store at Sycamore & Oak is ❸ THE MUSEUM DC, co-owned by LeGreg Harrison, the creative force behind Sycamore & Oak, and his partner Muhammed Hill. Their vibrant and recognizable logo is one of the earlier entrants into the DC streetwear and clothing-as-art realm, from sneakers to clothing to sunglasses. These gentlemen are on a mission to support and promote their own lines and other local fashion designers and original labels.

Next door to the creative complex is the ❹ ENTERTAINMENT AND SPORTS ARENA, home of the title-winning WNBA Mystics and the NBA G League Capital City Go-Go. The Mystics' devoted fans rock any arena where they play. Don your jersey and come out on a game day! Continue along Oak Street, where some of the former buildings of St E's have been or are in the process of being transformed into housing for people at all economic levels. Take a moment to admire these grand, Italian Renaissance Revival-style, red-brick buildings in an array of designs and layouts. The building between Poplar and Sycamore Streets SE is very intriguing. Though not much can easily be found about it, its uncommon shape and architectural design begs to be photographed.

Turn right onto Sycamore Street SE, passing the ❺ R.I.S.E. DEMONSTRATION CENTER. Built to be an incubator and training center for business ideas and innovations, it offers public, hands-on events for budding entrepreneurs. Continuing on, ❻ GATEWAY DC is an unconventional, angular greenspace and open-air pavilion that hosts concerts, farmers markets, and other community events. Walk up the inclined green roof and enjoy the view. Exit the campus via Cypress Street SE and cross MLK Avenue SE to ❼ PLAYERS LOUNGE, a local haunt for DC politicians and a favorite of "Mayor for Life" Marion Barry. Stop in for lunch or belly up to the bar and get to talking local politics with the regulars.

Turn right on MLK Avenue SE as you exit, ambling past old neighborhood businesses and services that are part of the fabric and the history of DC. The commercial section of numerous legacy businesses – those that have been here for decades – begins at Raleigh Street SE. This is where talking to strangers comes in handy as they all tell stories about their neighborhood. Now gone, Bob's Frozen Custard and the soda counter at People's Drugs were favorite destinations of those old enough to remember them. ❽ THE MLK DELI, the anchor of this block of retailers, serves up yummy sandwiches, many named for locals and DC cultural icons, like the Big Chair beef Reuben and Marion Barry salmon cakes.

Owner and storyteller Ray Kibler of ❾ MY 3 SONS UNISEX/BARBER SHOP is a lifelong resident, who has operated his shop for over 20 years. "The first thing people look for when they move to a neighborhood is a place to eat and a place to get a haircut," he says. Though his shop is more business than social center, he has a long relationship with his customers and knows most of the neighbors, elders, and fellow barbers and stylists within a few blocks. Each has their own clientele and their own ambience.

Seeing history through the lens of firehouses is a unique vantage point. Adjacent Chemical Engine 5 served from 1901 to 1913, covering locations where water hydrants were not yet installed. It was converted to ❿ ENGINE COMPANY 25, which for a time was the busiest firehouse in the city. It was the costliest and largest fire station of the day, and its construction heralded the development of the residential neighborhood around it. Locals speculated that its hilltop location helped the fire horses get to fires more quickly because they were running downhill.

Clockwise from top left: Inside Sycamore & Oak; Engine Company 25; Public art at Gateway DC; My 3 Sons Barber Shop

A ⓫ MURAL OF DOROTHY HEIGHT radiates brightly from the wall of the adjacent house. This force of nature was a key organizer of the 1963 March on Washington for Jobs and Freedom, and one of the most significant civil rights activists for generations. She was also renowned for the stunning, custom-made hats that she commissioned from local milliner Vanilla Bené. The portrait is by artist and history fanatic Kaliq Crosby, who states, "She has a lot of light, and I feel like you can understand her personality just from looking at my mural."

Step right across the avenue to the energetic ⓬ CONGRESS HEIGHTS ARTS + CULTURE CENTER (CHACC) whose mission is to focus on the exploration of arts and culture primarily within Black communities east of the Anacostia River and, as their website states, to "inspire, educate and expose the community, especially our youth, to arts, not only in our history but in our own community." Step inside to enjoy current exhibits, attend an event, and purchase locally created art. Just across 4th Street SE was once the home of the beloved Bob's Frozen Custard, known for their lemon custard. It was for decades the epicenter of the neighborhood and a destination for all Washingtonians.

Now fork right onto Alabama Avenue SW. Three blocks over, Lithuanian Jewish immigrants Ella and William Liff opened ⓭ LIFF'S MARKET in 1911. In 2002, the third generation sold it outside the family, but it remains the corner store here and the longest-running business in Congress Heights. The vivid murals on the building speak to the soul of the place.

Pride of place emanates from the local residents and business owners, who are the beating hearts of Congress Heights. Don't hesitate to strike up a conversation with anyone you meet along your walk to learn even more about this remarkable neighborhood.

Once you make your way back to the Metro station, take note of the series of five inter-connected Jewish cemeteries located across the avenue. Extend your walk by exploring the history in the gravestones.

Opposite: Kaliq Crosby's mural of Dorothy Height

CONGRESS HEIGHTS SE

❶ CHERRY BLOSSOM FENCE MURAL
1112 Oak Drive SE
Washington, DC 20032

❷ SYCAMORE & OAK RETAIL VILLAGE
1110 Oak Drive SE
Washington, DC 20032
www.sycamoreandoak.com

❸ THE MUSEUM DC
1110 Oak Drive SE, Suite 9
Washington, DC 20032
www.sycamoreandoak.com/the-museum

❹ ENTERTAINMENT AND SPORTS ARENA
1100 Oak Drive SE
Washington, DC 20032
www.eventsdc.com/venue/entertainment-and-sports-arena

❺ R.I.S.E. DEMONSTRATION CENTER
2730 Martin Luther King Jr. Avenue SE
Washington, DC 20032
stelizabethseast.com/rise-dc/about-rise

❻ GATEWAY DC
2700 Martin Luther King Jr. Avenue SE
Washington, DC 20032
www.eventsdc.com/venue/gateway-dc

❼ PLAYERS LOUNGE
2737 Martin Luther King Jr. Avenue SE
Washington, DC 20032

❽ THE MLK DELI
3113 Martin Luther King Jr. Avenue SE
Washington, DC 20032
www.themlkdeli.com

❾ MY 3 SONS UNISEX/ BARBER SHOP
3125 Martin Luther King Jr. Avenue SE
Washington, DC 20032

❿ ENGINE COMPANY 25
3203 Martin Luther King Jr. Avenue SE
Washington, DC 20032
historicsites.dcpreservation.org/items/show/1158

⓫ MURAL OF DOROTHY HEIGHT
3211 Martin Luther King Jr. Avenue SE
Washington, DC 20032
www.planning.dc.gov/cwprofiles

⓬ CONGRESS HEIGHTS ARTS + CULTURE CENTER (CHACC)
3200 Martin Luther King Jr. Avenue SE
Washington, DC 20032
www.chacc.org

⓭ LIFF'S MARKET
600 Alabama Avenue SE
Washington, DC 20032

Left: Congress Heights Arts Culture Center (CHACC)

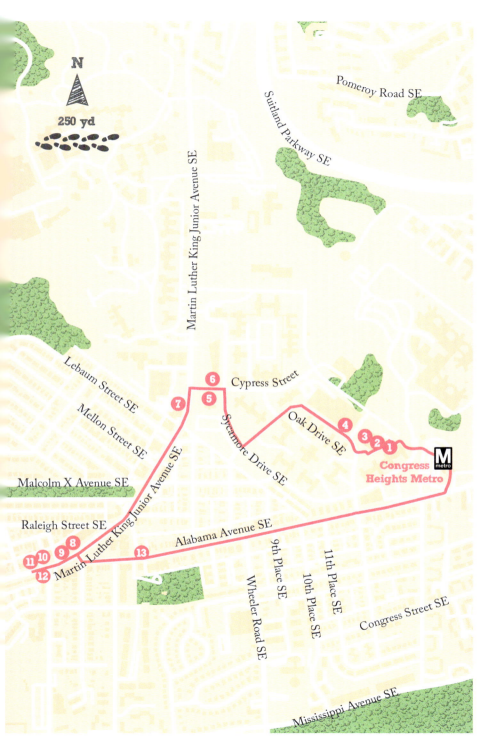

21 — Urban Renewal Design Walk

A neighborhood's roots before the bulldozers

> **BEST TIME:** Any season, any time of day
> **DISTANCE:** Approximately 2.5 miles
> **ROUTE DESCRIPTION:** Flat through crowded commercial and cozy residential areas
> **START:** Metro at L'Enfant Plaza (Blue, Green, Orange, Silver, Yellow Lines)
> **END:** Metro at Waterfront (Green Line)

Southwest is quite a contradictory area. It's part of Pierre L'Enfant's original plans and includes some of the oldest buildings in the city. But most of the buildings here are relatively new — by design.

In the early 20th century, Southwest was a poor area dotted with alley dwellings, a form of housing dating back as far as the Civil War. The alleys were largely occupied by African Americans and immigrant Jews. Mostly white civic leaders, however, saw the dwellings as a blight and successfully fought all the way to the Supreme Court to clear them under the power of eminent domain.

Until the 1950s, Southwest was Washington's largest working-class, waterfront neighborhood. To people like "America's Greatest Entertainer" Al Jolson, "First Lady of American Theatre" Helen Hayes, and Motown legend Marvin Gaye, it was home. Then, in one of the nation's first experiments in urban renewal, nearly all of Southwest was razed.

The plan was to replace them with modern buildings. Between 1954 and 1960, the government leveled 99% of the buildings here and forced 4,500 Black families to relocate. As a result, Southwest is full of mid-century modern buildings designed by architects who were attempting to create a new vision for urban living.

Opposite: Riverside Baptist Church

This walk takes you back to Southwest's early days and its rebirth as an urban utopia. Until 1801, fishermen sold their catch directly off their boats until the ❶ **MUNICIPAL FISH MARKET** was established. It remains the oldest continuously operating, open-air fish market in the US and is one of the few sites that survived the bulldozers.

Continue along the water, then left on 7th Street SW and cross Maine Avenue SW. The building with the stained-glass windows on the corner is ❷ **RIVERSIDE BAPTIST CHURCH,** established here in 1857. That year, the original property was purchased by the federal government under eminent domain. Using funds from the sale, the church purchased the current lot. The wave-inspired roof symbolizes the significance of water in the Baptist tradition, while simultaneously rooting the church to its neighborhood along the waterfront. The reuse of materials from the original building is also a powerful connection between the new church and its 160-year history in Southwest.

Turn right on Maine Avenue SW to 6th Street SW. ❸ **ARENA STAGE,** to the left, was the first racially integrated theater in DC and it helped start the regional theater movement. In 1960, Harry Weese (1915–1998), an American modernist architect who also designed the DC metro system, was hired to design one of the first modern in-the-round theaters in America, from which the theater company's name is derived. The theater was originally two separate buildings but when they needed more space, a third, smaller theater was added beneath a massive roof, creating a kind of three-ring circus under a big top.

Walk toward M Street SW, cross and continue on 6th Street SW. Go right onto 6th Street and head to the Tiber Island West building on the left at 490 M Street NW. Bear right and go toward the Anacostia Riverwalk Trail sign, then turn left. ❹ **TIBER ISLAND CO-OPERATIVE HOMES** is a collection of mid-rise apartment towers

Opposite: Municipal Fish Market

and clusters of townhouses. Developed in 1966, the complex is the result of a design competition won by a local firm and marked the beginning of DC's recognition as an incubator of first-rate architectural talent. Its name is derived from the name of a creek that was here long before the city of Washington, when this area was surrounded by water. The complex was the first condominium project built in DC and a model for the type of home ownership that is common today.

Tiber Island incorporates the 18th-century ❺ **THOMAS LAW HOUSE,** which functions as a community center. It's to the left across from Waterfront Park and is one of a handful of buildings to be spared the bulldozer. Built around 1794 or 1796, it's one of the city's oldest standing residences. Eliza Custis (1776–1831), the granddaughter of Martha Washington (1731–1802), lived here with her husband. It has been restored to resemble its original design and 18th-century character.

Ahead, the ❻ *TITANIC* **MEMORIAL** honors the men who gave their lives to save women and children during the sinking of the *Titanic* in 1912. The statue was designed by Gertrude Vanderbilt Whitney after a national fundraising effort by surviving widows from the disaster. The base and platform were designed by Henry Bacon (1866–1924), who also designed the Lincoln Memorial. Allegedly, the statue's pose was recreated by Leonardo DiCaprio and Kate Winslet in the hit film *Titanic* (1997). True or not, it's a heck of a story.

Turn left, and then at the corner of 4th and P Streets NW, turn left again. The barrel-roof townhouses and aluminum details of ❼ **RIVER PARK** aren't like anything else you'll see in DC. Designed by architect Charles M. Goodman (1906–1992), the complex was completed in 1962, the same year that *The Jetsons* first aired, which lends the buildings a techno-cool image of modernity. Reynolds Metals sponsored the project, hoping it would result in aluminum becoming the era's preferred roofing material, but that would not come to be.

Across the street, ❽ **HARBOUR SQUARE** was designed by Chloethiel Woodard Smith (1910–1992) and Daniel Urban Kiley (1912–2004), both of whom were principals in the reimagining of

Above: Arena Stage Below: Harbour Square apartment building

Clockwise from top left: Pearl Street; Thomas Law House; Southwest Duck Pond; *Titanic* Memorial

Southwest. In 1970, *Life* magazine called Smith one of the "Eight Women Who Made It [in a Man's World]." The complex has been home to a number of famous Washington residents, most notably Senator and later Vice President Hubert Humphrey. Supreme Court Justices Lewis M. Powell and David Souter also made Harbour Square their home, as did numerous senators and representatives.

Saved from destruction like Tiber Island, it integrates several older buildings. The ❾ **WHEAT ROW HOUSES** (1315, 1317, 1319, and 1321 4th Street SW) were built in 1794 by a group of developers called The Greenleaf Syndicate. Thomas Jefferson (1743–1826) was a house guest at one time. Even when they were built, the Georgian architectural style was considered out of date, and people found the houses "small and poorly constructed of inferior materials," according to the Miles 2 Go website. Yet here they remain more than 200 years later, a link to DC's earliest days.

Continue to M Street SW. Flanking the Waterfront-SEU Metro station are four identical apartment towers that look like Tetris blocks. They are all that remain of the Waterside shopping mall and office complex built in the early 1970s. The buildings were designed by famed architect I. M. Pei early in his career. Pei's contributions helped to shape Southwest as we know it and show early glimpses of his style, which would be refined in his design of the East Building of the National Gallery of Art and the glass "crystals" on the plaza.

Up 4th Street SW and across I Street SW is the ❿ POTOMAC PLACE TOWER complex on the right, the first structure to open in the new Southwest. It was designed by Chloethiel Woodard Smith, one of the visionary architects and planners who campaigned to start over again with a blank canvas. Critics noted the complex's inspiring views of the Capitol and Washington Monument. The building is also significant for its role in the landmark Supreme Court ruling that established eminent domain. Photographs of poor conditions in the area with the Capitol dome in the background set off the fervor to raze the area. Photos were even used in Soviet propaganda to illustrate "typical living conditions" in DC. When Soviet Premier Nikita Khrushchev visited in the late 1950s, President Eisenhower personally took him to see Potomac Place, then under construction, to illustrate the nation's housing progress.

Now double back on 4th Street SW to I Street SW, and turn right. Urban renewal planners valued public spaces. Completed in 1972, the ⓫ SOUTHWEST DUCK POND was built on a block that historically was known as Cow Alley, presumably for the cows that once wandered the packed-earth street and the alley dwellings that were common in the early 20th century.

The look of the pond was inspired by the Chesapeake Bay and Potomac River, and reflects the important connection between the District and its waterways, as evidenced by the prominence of the water feature. The pond is designed with a natural shoreline and edged with rocks from the rivers and native riparian plants. Today, red lounge chairs are clustered throughout the park and a Free Library offers reading material for anyone wanting to sit and enjoy a good book. The Southwest Business Improvement District hosts activities in the park, such as community dinners, live music, and holiday parties. More than a place just for nearby neighbors, it has become a destination location for everyone.

❶ MUNICIPAL FISH MARKET
1100 Maine Avenue SW
Washington, DC 20024
www.wharfdc.com/fish-market

❷ RIVERSIDE BAPTIST CHURCH
699 Maine Avenue SW
Washington, DC 20024
www.riversidedc.org

❸ ARENA STAGE
1101 6th Street SW
Washington, DC 20024
www.arenastage.org

❹ TIBER ISLAND COOPERATIVE HOMES
429 N Street SW
Washington, DC 20024
www.tiberisland.com

❺ THOMAS LAW HOUSE
corner of 6th and M Streets SW
Washington, DC 20024
www.tiberisland.com

❻ *TITANIC* MEMORIAL
Water & P Streets SW
Washington, DC 20024
www.nps.gov/places/000/titanic-memorial.htm

❼ RIVER PARK
Southeast corner of 4th & N Streets SW
Washington, DC 20024
www.riverparkdc.org

❽ HARBOUR SQUARE
N Street SW at 4th Street SW
Washington, DC 20024
www.harboursquare.coop

❾ WHEAT ROW HOUSES
1315, 1317, 1319, & 1321 4th Street SW
Washington, DC 20024
www.historicsites.dcpreservation.org/items/show/65

❿ POTOMAC PLACE TOWER
800 4th Street SW
Washington, DC 20024
www.monumentrealty.com/projects/potomac-place-towers

⓫ SOUTHWEST DUCK POND
6th & I Streets SW
Washington, DC 20024

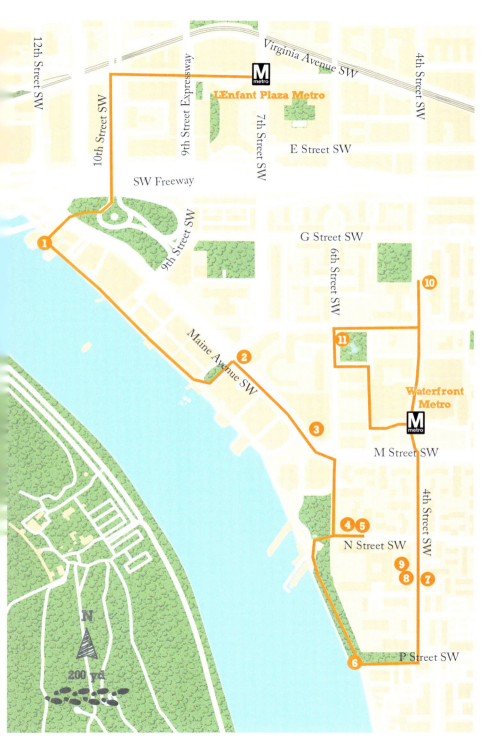

22 Wardman Architecture Walk

History behind the designs of famed DC architect

> **BEST TIME:** Any season, any time of day
> **DISTANCE:** Approximately 1 mile
> **ROUTE DESCRIPTION:** Flat and intimate through residential neighborhood
> **START:** Metro at Woodley Park-Zoo/Adams Morgan (Red Line)
> **END:** Metro at Woodley Park-Zoo/Adams Morgan or Cleveland Park (Red Line)

Situated on a peak arising from the valley of Rock Creek Park, Woodley Park originally attracted Washingtonians seeking relief from the summer heat and the hustle and bustle in downtown DC. The northwest neighborhood bears the indelible stamp of British-born Harry Wardman (1872–1938), one of the most influential local developers of the 20th century.

Starting out with modest row houses, Wardman's buildings grew in scope and luxury as the years went on. Many iconic apartments and hotels in Woodley are his creations, with the help of a variety of architects. The exclusive Hay-Adams and St. Regis Hotels, and the Wardman Tower, are the trifecta of iconic Wardman buildings. He was so prolific that when he died in 1938, 80,000 Washingtonians – one-tenth of the population – lived in houses and apartments he had built. Fortunately, many examples of his work still exist today, including several in the Woodley Park neighborhood.

The corner of Connecticut Avenue and Woodley Road NW is dominated by the historic ❶ **WARDMAN TOWER** to your left, the first of the renowned architect's buildings you'll encounter on this walk. It was built by Wardman in 1928 as an annex to the Ward-

Opposite: Wardman Tower

Above: Wardman homes Below: Party Animal statues at the Swiss Ambassador's residence

man Park Hotel, which used to stand adjacent to this imposingly elegant building.

When Wardman decided to add the luxury apartment tower, he tore down his own home to clear the property while his wife was visiting Paris. *Sacré bleu!* Designed by Mihran Mesrobian (1889–1975), a prominent architect who also helped design the aforementioned Hay-Adams and St. Regis Hotels, it is the only part of the old hotel still standing. Past residents include Presidents Dwight D. Eisenhower and Lyndon B. Johnson, FBI Director Herbert Hoover, and actress Marlene Dietrich. A few years ago, Wardman Tower made headlines by selling the city's second most expensive condo ever for $8.4 million!

Turn left onto Woodley Road NW. The first map of Woodley Park (dated 1875), then called Kervand's Woodley, shows Woodley Road (then called Woodley Lane) as the only road through the area and the heart of the new subdivision.

Next door to the Wardman Tower is where the Wardman Park Hotel was located. Built in 1917, the hotel was called "Wardman's Folly" because it was considered too far from downtown DC. Nevertheless, it was a huge success as soon as it opened. Modeled on the Homestead Resort in Virginia, it was the largest in the city, with 1,200 rooms, a dining room seating 500, a Turkish bath, a billiard room, a drugstore, and a grocery. Throughout World War II, Wardman Park was a bustling mini city of military generals, diplomats… and espionage. A British spy even operated out of the premises before the US entered World War II and helped change the course of the war. It was demolished in 1978 but historic photos show that the pair of Georgian Revival gates on the lawn once flanked either side of the hotel's semi-circular drive.

You can see examples of some early ❷ **WARDMAN HOMES** at 2651, 2653, 2657, and 2659 Woodley Road NW. He was particularly active in the development of Woodley Park and amassed a considerable fortune constructing speculatively here and elsewhere in the city. Busy throughout the first few decades of the 20th century, Wardman has arguably made a bigger impact on DC's residential real estate scene than any other developer. He got his start with modest row houses that defined the quintessential look of many local neighborhoods.

Even in this quiet area, you're bound to encounter a bit of a scandal – it is DC after all. In the 1920s, Alice Montague Warfield, Wallis Warfield Simpson's mother, ran a ❸ BOARDING HOUSE across the alley from the building that was originally built to house St. Thomas School. Wallis Simpson was an American socialite and double divorcée, who married Edward VIII of England and became the Duchess of Windsor. Their relationship created an international scandal that helped bring about his abdication from the British throne in 1936.

While much of DC is set in a regular grid pattern, historically Woodley Park was planned to have a winding street pattern. Because it was conceived as a residential retreat, it retains an elegant feel that is conducive to unhurried strolls. Your walk along Woodley Road NW follows parts of the original Woodley Lane route that residents, including Harry Wardman himself, traversed in the late 1870s.

Walk to 29th Street NW and turn right. As you go along, look over at the gated expanse to your left. The avant-garde design of the ❹ SWISS AMBASSADOR'S RESIDENCE, built on the Swiss Embassy compound, stands in architectural opposition to the residential homes around it. Its black and white exterior is supposedly inspired by the rugged, snow-capped Swiss Alps. And no, your eyes aren't playing tricks on you – there really are a donkey and elephant on the embassy's grounds. Well, sculptures of them anyway. These Party Animals are hold-overs from DC's largest public art project in 2002.

Turn left on Cathedral Avenue NW. ❺ THE MARET SCHOOL, also known as Woodley Mansion, was built in 1801 by Phillip Barton Key, uncle of Francis Scott Key, composer of "The Star Spangled Banner." He called the house "Woodley" after Woodley House in England, where he had spent some time. He liked the look of the place and stipulated that his mansion should be of a similar design.

Opposite: Woodley Park is named after this former estate.

The neighborhood that grew up around it took its name from this estate.

Another example of a Wardman house stands to your right at 2937 Cathedral Avenue NW. According to an advertisement in *The Evening Star* archives, the former exhibit home was priced at $17,500 in 1925, which is about $245,000 today. In 2024, the home was valued at $1.4 million.

Backtrack on Cathedral Avenue NW and go left on 29th Street NW. If it suddenly feels like you've entered an English village, that's by design. Among Wardman's famous projects was one he called the ❻ ENGLISH VILLAGE in 1923. Wardman was an Englishman, so perhaps he was recreating a bit of home. Houses in this area mirror the popular Tudor and English garden aesthetics popular during the era. The homes also incorporated what was an emerging necessity at the time: the garage.

This development was the first project Wardman's frequent collaborator, architect Mihran Mesrobian, designed in the United States. Mesrobian created palaces during the twilight of the Turkish sultans and was rescued from a Turkish prison by Thomas Edward Lawrence (1888–1935), aka Lawrence of Arabia, before coming to America. Now head back to Cathedral Avenue NW, turn left and go to Connecticut Avenue NW.

Designed and developed by Wardman and Mesrobian in 1922, ❼ SOUTH CATHEDRAL MANSIONS, on the corner, was part of Wardman's vision for luxury living in the area. Originally called the Five Courts Mansion in planning documents, it used the name "mansions" to reference English landscape architecture. The complex contains three separate buildings, each with similar but distinct architecture that complemented one another. Built in the Classical Revival style, it contains open landscaping meant to blend the man-made structures with the natural scenery found in the city. The buildings increased the ability for more people to live and work in

Opposite: South Cathedral Mansions

the city, and its location on Connecticut Avenue NW made it an optimal stop for the city's streetcar system. Despite the project's success, Wardman suffered financial problems and declared bankruptcy in 1931. Cathedral Mansions remained steadfast and changed hands over the decades.

① WARDMAN TOWER
2660 Woodley Road NW
Washington, DC 20008
www.wardmantower.com

② WARDMAN HOMES
2651–2659 Woodley Road NW
Washington, DC 20008

③ ALICE MONTAGUE WARFIELD BOARDING HOUSE
2703 Woodley Road NW
Washington, DC 20008

④ SWISS AMBASSADOR'S RESIDENCE
2900 Cathedral Avenue NW
Washington, DC 20008
www.eda.admin.ch/countries/usa/en/home/representations/embassy-washington.html

⑤ THE MARET SCHOOL
3000 Cathedral Avenue NW
Washington, DC 20008
www.maret.org

⑥ HARRY WARDMAN'S "ENGLISH VILLAGE"
29th Street NW
Washington, DC 20008

⑦ SOUTH CATHEDRAL MANSIONS
2900 Connecticut Avenue NW
Washington, DC 20008

Below: Wardman's "English Village"

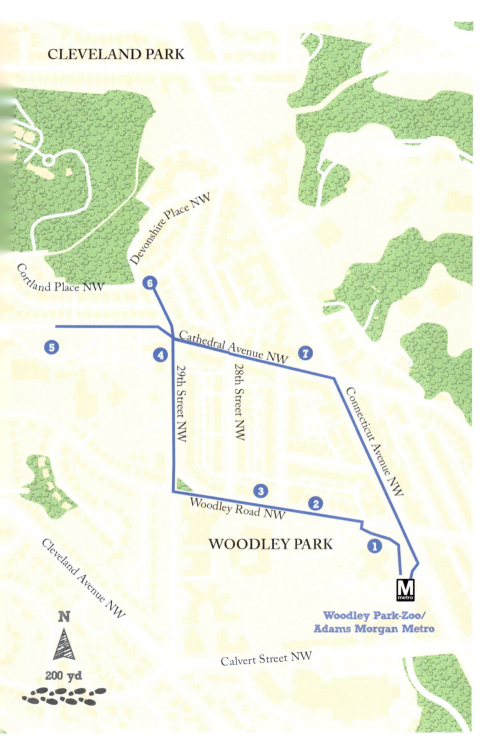

Acknowledgements

Paige Muller
Thank you to my co-author, Andrea Seiger, for her sage advice and willingness always to go on an adventure. If we ever do a podcast together, we're calling it "Kill Your Darlings!" To David Blum, librarian and dear friend, thank you for your love of knowledge and saying "yes" to my invites to explore DC with endless enthusiasm. Thanks to Steve Knight at the Art Deco Society of Washington for telling stories through architecture that bring the history of DC's neighborhoods alive. I am deeply grateful to Elizabeth Nelson and Beth Purcell at the Capitol Hill Restoration Society for their expertise and for guiding me to the right information I didn't know I needed. I am indebted to the librarians and the access to the many free resources at the DC Public Library that helped inform this book and give it substance. Huge thanks to the incredible photographer for this book – Shedrick Pelt – for lovingly capturing a side of DC not many people get to see. Finally, to Jason Booms for his invaluable feedback, encouragement, and decades of stalwart friendship and support.

Andrea Seiger
I want to thank all of the storytellers and neighbors who shared insights about their beloved corners of the city. They enlightened me and made me explore even more, through their eyes and with their narratives for inspiration. There is always a conversation to be had with a stranger or a friend, and to these lovely people I am particularly grateful. To Paige Muller, my partner in walks and poking around DC, with whom I am always in search of something new to us. To Shedrick Pelt for the uncommon eye he has for our city. Ray Kibler of My 3 Sons Barber Shop; Chief Greene of Sycamore & Oak; and Reek of The Museum for the long conversations about the love they have for Congress Heights, their neighbors, and small business owners, and why they all nurture or return to their roots there. AJ Orlikoff, Dayle Dooley, for sharing their favorite stories of Native Americans in Congressional Ce-

metery. Aona Jefferson, whose stories of educators inspired my own walks in Deanwood. Marisol at Corado's in Adams Morgan, who gave me recipes to feed my cravings. Jeffrey Neher and Ryan Shaw of the Petworth Public Library for their enthusiasm about this book and their branch being included. Concierge Brian Thomasson at the Hay-Adams Hotel for a hilarious exchange of DC hotel stories. Anthony Olweny and his husband for the joy they bring with the Neon House. And to Derek Gray for the many talks about a broad array of stories of the city, and Mark Greek and their colleagues in the People's Archive at Martin Luther King Jr. Library, who all aided and abetted my seemingly endless use of the archive to seek out stories.

Shedrick Pelt
I'll start by saying I am nothing without the people who love me and the community that keeps me safe. Thank you to my family: Pops, Ma-Dukes, Dizzy, Bre, Renee, and Celeste, whose unwavering support and inspiration mean the world to me. To the talented authors of this book, Paige Muller and Andrea Seiger, I am deeply grateful for your faith in my contributions. To DC, a city I've fallen head over heels for, thank you for allowing me the space to grow. And to all those striving to build a better future for humanity, remember that you are not alone. ROLL TIDE ROLL!

The information in this book was accurate at the time of publication, but it may change at any time. Please confirm the details for the places you're planning to visit before you head out on your adventures.

Paige Muller is a global citizen who has lived in South America, Japan, and England, and now calls Washington, DC home. She is the owner of Curious Caravan, a boutique company specializing in off-the-beaten-path adventures in the District. She can usually be found in the front row of a local concert, checking out an experimental art show, or taking a walkabout to discover murals and new nooks and crannies. Her website is: curious-caravan.com, and follow her DC adventures on social at @curious-caravan.com.

Andrea Seiger is a curious explorer and tour guide, and in her career in tourism and meetings management she has had many unique DC and international adventures. Road tripping is her biggest joy, and she is prone to walking into entryways to mysterious interiors and exploring the uncommon everywhere she goes. She authored *111 Places in Washington That You Must Not Miss*, and her list of places yet to visit in DC and the world is a constant companion. In her spare time, she runs her small business, Urban Safari, for which she creates off-the-beaten-path tours to intriguing locations in the US and abroad.

Shedrick Pelt is a creative professional based in Washington, DC. Originally from Huntsville, Alabama and with a background rooted in Harlem, New York, he is dedicated to fostering culture and community. Pelt's work is situated at the intersection of time and place, allowing him to delve into intricate conversations and themes while embodying a role akin to that of a historian. With over a decade of experience, he specializes in photojournalism, portraiture, music, and commercial photography.